LAYER BY LAYER

LAYER BY LAYER

COLLAGE PROJECTS
FOR HOME DECORATING

Martingale®
& COMPANY

Layer by Layer: Collage Projects for Home Decorating

© 2004 by Martingale & Company

Martingale & Company
20205 144th Avenue NE
Woodinville, WA 98072-8478 USA
www.martingale-pub.com

CREDITS

President ◆ Nancy J. Martin

CEO ◆ Daniel J. Martin

Publisher ◆ Jane Hamada

Editorial Director ◆ Mary V. Green

Managing Editor ◆ Tina Cook

Technical Editor ◆ Dawn Anderson

Copy Editor ◆ Melissa Bryan

Design Director ◆ Stan Green

Illustrator ◆ Laurel Strand

Cover and Text Designer ◆ Shelly Garrison

Photographer ◆ Bill Lindner

Photo Assistants ◆ Jason Lund and Tom Heck

Photo Stylist ◆ Bridget Haugh

Printed in China

09 08 07 06 05 04   8 7 6 5 4 3 2 1

**Library of Congress
Cataloging-in-Publication Data**

Layer by layer: collage projects for home decorating.
        p. cm.
    ISBN 1-56477-542-9
    1. Collage. 2. House furnishings. I. Martingale & Company.
    TT910.L39 2004
    702'.81'2—dc22

                    2004003595

MISSION STATEMENT
Dedicated to providing quality products
and service to inspire creativity.

CONTENTS

INTRODUCTION

There is something undeniably unique about the layered look—it instantly evokes a sense of romance and nostalgia. Blending images in a patchwork fashion creates a sophisticated style that you may think is tricky to duplicate. But don't be fooled! With the projects in *Layer by Layer*, you can achieve that luxurious layered look while having lots of fun along the way.

The fun starts with choosing which images to layer. This project collection features a range of images, some with an old-world charm and some with a more modern feel. You can use simple torn pieces of handmade paper, premade decorative papers and stickers, vintage-style labels, precut wallpaper images, or even maps and postcards from a memorable vacation. Follow the suggestions in the book, or dream up your own ideas to make your projects truly unique.

After selecting your images, you will discover that for most projects a little cutting and gluing is all it takes to master the art of collage and decoupage. Try the techniques on a wistful Love Letter Pillow, a Butterfly Bath Chest, or a Stenciled Mirror Frame. Create a table runner filled with rose engravings, a French Memo Board to organize your everyday papers, or a Floral Paper Lampshade to add a dreamy quality to a bedroom. You can even get whimsical with Framed Chicken and Rooster Collages! Your creativity with charms, threads, page pebbles, paper flowers, and ribbons can further enhance your work.

From projects featuring a feminine touch to designs with retro appeal, you'll find home-decor projects to please friends, family, and especially yourself. Start layer by layer and watch your projects come to life!

COLLAGE WASTEBASKET

By Saralyn Ewald, Creative Coordinator, Archiver's: The Photo Memory Store

Let this wastebasket with its reproductions of vintage soap and perfume labels add charm to your home or office. A simple wooden wastebasket is covered with torn pieces of paper featuring musical notes and then bordered with a pointed band of black and taupe diamonds and black braid trim. The labels, graced with elegant floral motifs, are adhered at various angles around the center of the wastebasket to add a touch of whimsy. The basket is also lined with torn pieces of lavender paper, adding to its feminine appeal.

MATERIALS

- Wooden wastebasket, 8" x 8" x 10½"
- 3 sheets of 12" x 12" paper for background (music/Eiffel Tower pattern from the ScrappyChic Vintage Collection, Book 2, by Me and My Big Ideas)
- 2 sheets of 12" x 12" paper for border (black/taupe diamond pattern from the ScrappyChic Scrapbook Paper Collection, Book 1, by Me and My Big Ideas) cut to:
  - 4 pieces, 4¼" x 8"
  - 4 pieces, 2" x 8"
- 5 sheets of 12" x 12" paper for interior (lavender Floral Script pattern by Sandylion Sticker Designs)
- 1 piece of 5" x 10" bright white watercolor paper, cold press 140lb. (Arches)
- 4 pieces of 4¼" x 8" light-colored cardstock
- 5 or 6 reproductions of vintage soap and perfume labels (ScrappyChic Ephemera Assortments 2, 8, and 11 by Me and My Big Ideas)
- 1½ yards of black braid trim
- Mod Podge, matte (Plaid)
- pH Neutral PVA Adhesive (Books By Hand)
- Super 77 Spray Adhesive (3M)
- Wonder Tape, ⅛" width (Suze Weinberg)

TOOLS AND SUPPLIES

- Foam brush
- Kraft paper
- Metal ruler
- Self-healing cutting mat
- X-Acto knife

INSTRUCTIONS

1. Tear the music-motif background paper into asymmetrical pieces no smaller than 2" x 2" and no larger than 5" x 5". Cover a work surface with kraft paper and place the wastebasket on the paper. Cover the outside of the wastebasket with the torn paper pieces, securing them in place with spray adhesive; place the pieces at various angles, wrapping paper around the sides and overlapping the edges. Allow the paper to run off the bottom edges of the wastebasket, but stop about 1½" from the top of the wastebasket, because the diamond-patterned border, applied later, will cover that area.

2. Use an X-Acto knife to trim the excess paper from around the feet of the wastebasket.

3. Use spray adhesive to adhere three to four vintage labels around the center of the wastebasket, on top of the music pattern, overlapping the edges of some labels and wrapping some around the corners onto a second side. Leave space for two additional labels, which will be added later. Use the collage plan on page 11 as a guide for placement.

4. Apply a thin, even coat of Mod Podge to the outside of the wastebasket, using a foam brush and working in vertical strokes. Allow to dry, and then apply a second coat of Mod Podge in the same manner. Allow wastebasket to dry completely.

⇒ DESIGNER'S TIP ⇐

To reuse your foam brush, be sure to wash it promptly after each use.

5. Use spray adhesive to adhere two vintage labels to watercolor paper. Using an X-Acto knife, ruler, and self-healing cutting mat, carefully cut out the labels and set them aside.

6. Glue the 4¼" x 8" pieces of diamond-patterned paper for border to the pieces of cardstock, matching edges and using spray adhesive. Photocopy or trace the border pattern on page 12 and cut out. Position the pattern on the back of a border piece (cardstock side) and trace. Repeat for the remaining three border pieces. Using an X-Acto knife, ruler, and self-healing cutting mat, cut along the marked pattern lines on each border piece. Set border pieces aside.

7. Tear the lavender paper for the interior of the wastebasket into asymmetrical pieces no smaller than 2" x 2" and no larger than 5" x 5". Using spray adhesive, cover the inside of the wastebasket with the torn pieces. The straight edges of the paper can be aligned with the top inside edges of the wastebasket.

8. Apply a thin, even coat of Mod Podge to the inside of the wastebasket, using a foam brush and working in vertical strokes. Allow to dry, and then apply a second coat of Mod Podge in the same manner.

9. Apply a thin layer of pH Neutral PVA Adhesive across the top edge of one side of the wastebasket. Carefully apply a 2" x 8" diamond-patterned piece, covering the glued top edge but not overlapping the inside of the wastebasket. Allow excess paper to hang over the front. Smooth out any air bubbles across the top, and then allow the glue to set for a few minutes. Apply glue to the rest of the paper and smooth the paper down, attaching it to the front of the wastebasket. Allow excess paper to extend past the corner edges until the glue has dried.

10. Trim any excess paper from the corners of the wastebasket with an X-Acto knife. Repeat the papering process for the remaining three top edges of the wastebasket, working on one edge at a time.

11. Apply a thin layer of pH Neutral PVA Adhesive to the back of one of the diamond-patterned border pieces. Carefully apply the piece to one side of the wastebasket, aligning the straight edge with the top edge of the basket and overlapping the previously placed diamond-patterned piece. Allow the excess paper to extend past the sides, and smooth out any air bubbles. Allow the glue to dry at least 10 minutes, and then use an X-Acto knife to trim any excess paper from the corner edges of the wastebasket. Repeat the process for the remaining border pieces, working on one side at a time.

12. Apply a single line of Wonder Tape around each side of the wastebasket, positioned approximately 1¼" below the upper edge. Remove the backing from the tape.

13. Attach the black braid trim to the tape, applying pressure to secure it in place. Trim off the excess where the ends meet. Cover the ends with a small amount of pH Neutral glue to prevent fraying.

14. Using Wonder Tape, secure the last two vintage labels from step 5 to the wastebasket, using the collage plan below as a guide.

⋛ Designer's Tip ⋜

The diamond-patterned border and the two paper-backed vintage labels are not coated with Mod Podge on this project, in order to provide textural contrast between the surfaces. If your wastebasket will be in a high-traffic area, you may wish to coat all surfaces with Mod Podge for added protection.

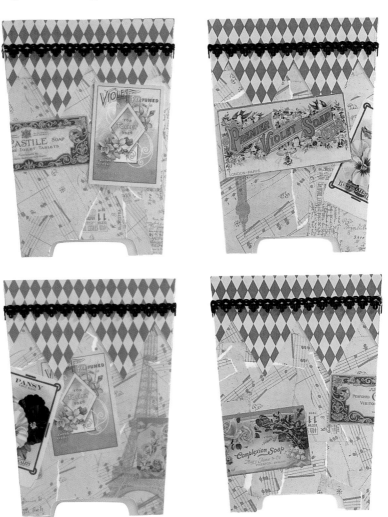

Collage Plan

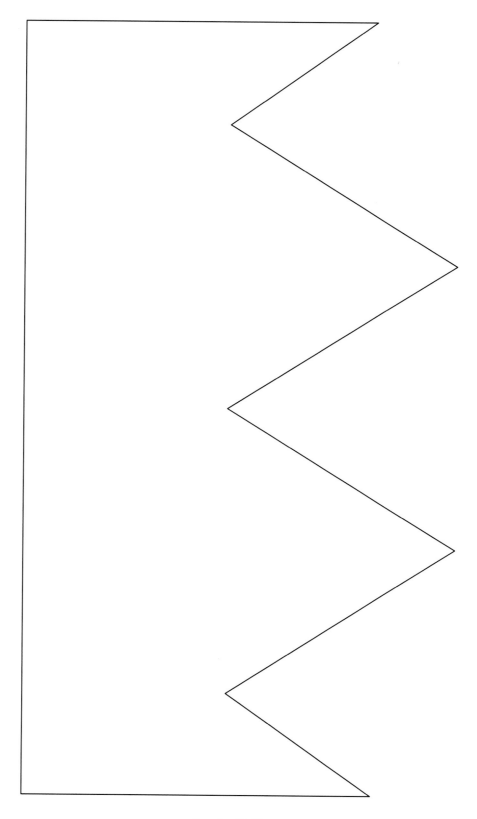

Border Pattern

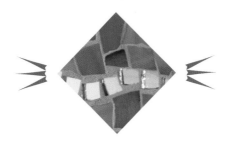

MOSAIC MIRROR WITH SHELF

By Jill MacKay

One is reminded of old-world charm by this collage project. Its beauty comes from a variety of glass, tile, and mirror materials—even recycled china. The borders were created from a set of second-hand china plates featuring gold detailing, along with tile purchased in a similar color. Coordinating with the sage green and gold of the china are fragments of "ring mottle" stained glass, a style of stained glass first made popular by Tiffany. It is characterized by ring-like effects resulting from a mix of colors throughout the glass—in this case pinks, greens, and ambers. Gold and rose-colored mirror pieces, glass gems in both frosted and iridescent tones, and yellow ceramic leaves all appear as accents.

MATERIALS

- Mirror-and-shelf unit with three utility hooks, total dimensions approximately 13½" x 21"
- 17 sage and gold china saucers, 4" in diameter
- 7 sage green ceramic tiles, 4" x 4"
- 8" x 12" piece of ring mottle stained glass (pinks, light greens, and ambers)
- 7" x 12" piece of rose-colored mirror
- 6" x 12" piece of gold mirror
- 4 small pastel green frosted glass gems with flat backs (available in packages of 25 mosaic marbles by Plaid)
- 2 large amber iridescent glass gems
- 14 small light yellow ceramic leaves
- 2 large light yellow ceramic leaves

- 2 cut-glass cabinet knobs
- 1 single brass hook
- 2-oz. bottle of liquid pure pigment in green (Createx)
- Two 1-lb. cartons of white sanded grout (Plaid)

TOOLS AND SUPPLIES

- 2 disposable containers or small buckets (for grouting)
- 4-oz. tube of clear silicone adhesive
- Black permanent marker
- Breaking pliers
- Ceramic tile nippers
- Craft sticks
- Dust mask
- Glass cutter
- Masking tape
- Mosaic glass cutters (Plaid)
- Paper plates
- Plastic (to cover work surface)
- Polishing cloth (soft material, such as an old T-shirt, not terry cloth)
- Razor blade
- Rubber gloves
- Ruler
- Safety glasses
- Screwdriver
- Sponge

Note: Most stained glass and mirror is sold in sheets 12" x 12" or larger. The sizes listed on page 13 are the actual amounts of these materials used in this project.

The number of china pieces you will need is going to depend on the size of your mirror and the size of the plates you purchase (that is, saucers vs. dinner plates). The amount listed reflects what was used for this project. It might be wise to buy a little more than you think you will need, just to be on the safe side. I purchased 30 pieces all from the same set of china, and this thrift-store bargain cost just $9.00. Most of the pieces were the size of saucers or pie plates, and although there was quite a bit left over, it can be saved for future projects.

⇒ DESIGNER'S TIPS ⇐

- Always wear safety goggles while cutting or nipping glass, mirror, or tile.

- You will find that fitting odd-shaped pieces together gets easier and easier. The more you do it, the more you will develop an "eye" for it. You'll learn to spot the shape you need, and the amount of extra nipping and refining you do will decrease. It's like putting a puzzle together, looking for the piece that's just the right shape.

- Take the time to cut up your materials before you begin. With all the basic cutting done beforehand, this project will go together much faster. Trimming the china down to size will depend on the dimensions of the mirror-and-shelf unit you purchased. The unit used for this project has a frame with a working space 2" wide. The china was trimmed down to ¾" to allow room for a nice inlaid band of ceramic tile. Trim your china so you leave enough room for a band of tile that is equal to or greater in size than the china border. Anything smaller will be too difficult to work with. Once you have a piece of china nipped down to the size that you desire, place it on an even surface to make sure it lies flat. It should not rock back and forth at all, as any curvature of the piece can interfere with secure adhesion. If there is any rocking, continue nipping the piece until it lies flat.

- When gluing, I recommend that you spread the glue around on the surface of the wood with the nozzle tip of the glue tube. Make sure there is enough glue to securely adhere the mosaic piece to the surface, but not so much that when you press it firmly in place the glue squishes up and fills the spaces between the pieces. These spaces are for the grout. Use a craft stick to clear away any extra glue that has oozed out. The spaces between pieces should be approximately ¹⁄₁₆" wide or slightly larger, and should be kept fairly consistent throughout the project.

Instructions

1. Remove the utility hooks that came on the front of the mirror-and-shelf unit, and replace them with the cut-glass knobs and brass hook to add to the collage effect.

2. Use the glass cutter to score the gold mirror into narrow strips, approximately 5/16" wide and running the length of the sheet. Use the breaking pliers to snap off each individual strip. Then, holding each strip over a paper plate, use the mosaic glass cutters to nip the strips into small squares and rectangles, approximately 1/4" to 5/16" long. Do not measure here—just "eyeball" your cuts, as differences in size and shape will actually make the pieces more interesting to look at. Over a second paper plate, continue using the mosaic glass cutters to nip the ring mottle stained glass into random-sized shapes and shards. Do the same with the rose-colored mirror over yet another paper plate. Carefully use the mosaic glass cutters to cut the china plates in half, then in half again, and then nip each quarter into eighths. Next nip all interior portions off each plate piece until you are left with just the decorative rim. Prepare all the china in this way. Use the ceramic tile nippers to nip up two or three of the ceramic tiles into shapes and shards of different sizes. You don't need to nip all the tile, as you may not need to use it all. You can always nip up more if necessary.

3. To position the small green gems, measure to the halfway point on each of the four sides of the frame and make a mark on the inside edge. (Note: The frame shown had an inner edge of natural wood that was left undecorated. Your unit may or may not allow you this option.) Using the clear silicone adhesive, glue a gem in place at each of these marks, making sure the gems do not extend past the edge. Again using the silicone adhesive, glue

the ceramic leaf decorations in place, referring to the detail photos for placement. The decorations on the upper and lower borders of the frame consist of one large ceramic leaf and two smaller leaves. The decorations on the left and right sides of the frame consist only of three small leaves.

Leaf Decorations for Top and Bottom Borders

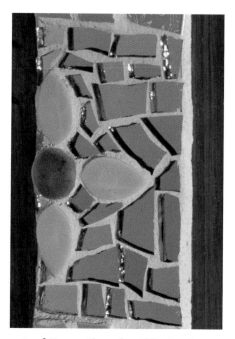

Leaf Decorations for Side Borders

4. On one of the leaf designs, measure 1/2" away from the tip of one of the leaves that runs along the inner edge of the frame, and use the marker to draw a line across the width of the frame. Do this on each side of all four leaf

designs. Then glue the rose-colored mirror shards to the frame to fill in the space within these lines, creating rose-colored rectangles around the leaf decorations. Nip and shape the glass with mosaic glass cutters when necessary to fit the space. Refer to the collage plan on page 18 and to the project photo for placement. The project as shown also uses rose-colored mirror fragments to decorate the inside edges of the support arms below the shelf. If your unit has similar support arms, fill in these areas without letting any of the mirror shards extend out over the edges.

5. Glue the large amber glass gems to the front surface of the support arms, about ¼" above the bottom edge, one on each side. (If your unit does not have support arms, simply glue the gems to the front of the area below the shelf, on either side of the decorative knobs.) Referring to the collage plan, use the marker to draw wavy lines extending above each of the large glass gems and also to the left and right of the upper and lower leaf decorations on the frame. Glue the small gold mirror squares in place on each of the wavy lines.

6. Use the stained glass shards to fill in the remaining spaces around the wavy lines on the upper and lower portions of the frame, as well as around the large glass gems. Nip and shape the shards with the mosaic glass cutters to fit where necessary.

7. Glue a row of china to both the left and right sides of the frame, facing the smooth edge of the china pieces outward. Place a row of china on the surface side of the shelf running along the outside edge, as well as in two rows above and below the glass knobs and brass hook (with the smooth edge of the china facing downward in each row). Refer to the collage plan for placement if needed.

8. Fill in the remaining areas on the frame and the section around the knobs and hook by gluing on odd-shaped shards of ceramic tile, shaping with the tile nipper to fit when needed. On the remaining shelf area, use two rows of larger rectangular pieces to create a smooth surface for setting things on. Let dry overnight.

9. Cover your work surface with plastic in preparation for grouting. Next clean the entire surface of the mosaic design, using a craft stick or razor blade to scrape off any residual glue from the glass, tile, or mirror. Use masking tape to cover any exposed wood so grout will not get into its pores and discolor it. On the project as shown, the inner and side wooden edges of the frame were left undecorated, as were the edge and underside of the shelf. These areas all need to be covered with tape. Carefully place the tape's edge right next to the edge of the mosaic work, butting the two up against each other but making sure not to cover any of the mosaic pieces. Once you have the placement of the tape exactly where you want it, smooth it down with your fingertips to make sure no grout can sneak under it.

10. Put on the dust mask and pour one and a half pounds of grout into one of the containers; fill the other with water. Add two drops of green pure pigment to the dry grout. Following the manufacturer's instructions, add water and mix the grout thoroughly until it is an even color and is the consistency of thick oatmeal. If you want to make the color more intense, simply add another drop of pigment. If the consistency becomes too thin or watery, simply mix in additional dry grout. Apply the grout over the entire surface of the mosaic design. Using gloved fingertips, firmly

press the grout down into the crevices. Along the outside and inside edges you will want to carefully smooth these grout lines with your fingertips. Make sure these spaces are filled but that the grout doesn't overlap the tape, or when you remove the tape it will pull the grout off with it. You can use a craft stick to carefully scrape the grout off the tape, almost like carving an edge.

11. Wet the sponge in water, wringing out the excess. Begin to clean the mosaic work by sponging away the excess grout, but take care not to wipe away too much grout. You may need to go back and fix the lines along the edges if small amounts of the grout became dislodged by the sponge. Just add a little more grout with your fingertips and smooth again. Let dry 10 to 15 minutes, and polish clean with a soft cloth. Very carefully and slowly remove all the masking tape. Repair any spots where the grout may have come loose by reapplying small amounts of wet grout, and then clean and polish the repaired spots again. Let the piece dry overnight.

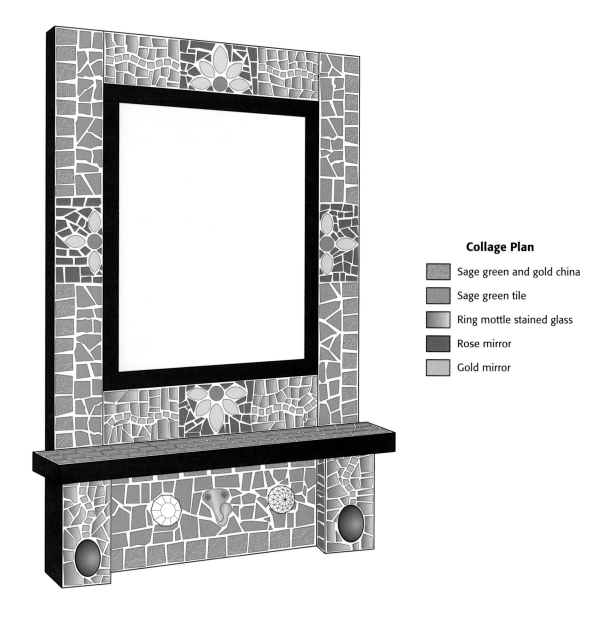

Collage Plan

Sage green and gold china

Sage green tile

Ring mottle stained glass

Rose mirror

Gold mirror

BUTTERFLY BATH CHEST

By Christine Falk

Create this beautiful chest for organizing small items in the bathroom. Use it to store hair clips, bandages, soaps, medicines, or other necessities. Start with an unfinished chest and paint the outside a dusty green, except for the drawer fronts, which are embellished with decorative papers, stickers, butterfly images, and postage stamps. Add decorative butterfly cabinet knobs that are finished with a soft verdigris wash in the same green as the paint color.

MATERIALS

- Wooden chest with 6 drawers, total dimensions 11¼" x 11¼" x 8" deep
- Acrylic paint in Cactus Green (Delta Ceramcoat)
- Tan-colored mulberry paper
- Two 8½" x 11" sheets of cream-colored copy paper or cardstock
- Scrapbooking paper in a variety of script, music, and travel motifs (Patterns 1901, 1902, 1906, 1912, 1916, 1918, 1919, and 1921 from the French Collection by 7 Gypsies)
- Fern sticker ("Life's Journey Pansies" by K and Company)
- Tag stickers ("Life's Journey Always Tags" by K and Company)
- Letter stickers ("Aged Typewriter" from the Nostalgiques collection by Rebecca Sower)
- 2 recycled postage stamps (The Herbarium)
- 2 butterfly images (from *Old-Time Butterfly Vignettes in Full Color*, selected and arranged by Carol Belanger Grafton, Dover Publications)
- 6 butterfly drawer pulls with screws
- Artsy Collage Decoupage and Collage Gel
- Interior matte finish varnish (Delta Ceramcoat)

TOOLS AND SUPPLIES

- Access to a color photocopy machine or access to a computer, color printer, and scanner
- Drill and drill bit for making holes for cabinet knobs, if necessary
- Fiskars Paper Edgers, deckle pattern
- 3 foam brushes
- Metal ruler
- Paintbrush, ⅜" flat
- Paper towels
- Pencil
- Sandpaper (100-grit and 220-grit)
- Scissors
- Screwdriver
- Spray mister
- Wood filler
- Wood sealer

INSTRUCTIONS

1. Remove the drawers from the chest. If your chest has cabinet knobs attached to the drawers, remove them as well. Fill any imperfections in the wood chest with wood filler and allow to dry. Sand the chest lightly with 100-grit sandpaper. Remove the sanding dust with a damp paper towel. Using a foam brush, seal the wood with wood sealer.

2. Using a new foam brush, paint the top, bottom, and sides of the chest green. Use the flat brush to paint the chest front. Paint the chest with a second coat of paint as before. Allow the chest to dry. Sand the chest lightly with 220-grit sandpaper. Remove the sanding dust with a damp paper towel. Apply a third coat of paint as before and let dry.

3. Using a color photocopier, photocopy the word "WASH" (above right) and the desired butterfly images (the project shown used two with green tones) onto cream-colored paper. Or, on a computer, type the word "WASH" in capital letters using the Algerian font in

22-point size and print it in brown ink onto cream-colored paper. Scan the desired butterfly images and print them onto paper using a color printer. Set aside the word and butterflies.

WASH

4. Remove any existing handles from the chest drawers and either discard or save them for another project. Place a drawer, front side down, on the wrong side of a piece of scrapbooking paper and trace around the drawer. Cut ¼" beyond the marked line. Trim away a ¼" square at each corner as shown. Repeat for each drawer, using the same paper pattern.

Trim away ¼" square at each corner.

Apply decoupage gel to the back of one of the papers. Position the paper on a drawer front and fold the edges of the paper around the edges of the drawer front. Repeat for the remaining drawers.

5. Cut other patterned papers and the mulberry paper in various sizes and shapes, tearing some edges for an elegantly imperfect look. Apply papers to the drawer fronts randomly with decoupage gel, overlapping to create a collage effect.

6. Cut the word "WASH" to fit under the frame sticker from the set of tag stickers, as shown.

Glue the word "WASH" to the bottom left corner of the bottom left drawer. Place the frame sticker over it so that the word appears in the opening.

7. Cut out the butterfly images. Using decoupage gel, apply postage stamps and butterfly images to the drawer fronts, referring to the project photo for placement. For the middle drawer on the right side, first mount the postage stamp onto a 1½" x 2½" piece of scrapbooking paper cut out with a decorative paper edger. Place the fern, tag,

and letter stickers spelling "BATH" on the drawer fronts, referring to the project photo for placement.

8. Apply matte finish varnish to the chest and drawer fronts, following the manufacturer's directions. Allow to dry for 24 hours.

9. If the drawers on your chest do not have holes for cabinet knobs, hold a ruler diagonally across each drawer front and mark the center with a pencil. Drill holes at the marked points. Attach the butterfly knobs to the chest.

ROSE ENGRAVINGS TABLE RUNNER

By Genevieve A. Sterbenz

Grace your table with this elegant runner embellished with black engraving designs. The designs are added using photo transfer paper and a household iron. The focal design appears to be only one image, but it is actually layered—a combination of different engravings. To finish the runner, add a border with detailed scrollwork and cherubs.

The layering process for the focal design is most easily done on a computer with a graphics program such as Adobe Photoshop. If you do not have access to a computer, you can use a photocopy machine to resize the different elements of the design, and then you can cut and paste them together. Print out a copy to test the design. When you are satisfied, create a mirror image on the copy machine and follow the manufacturer's directions to print it out onto the transfer paper. Most often your local copy center will be willing to create the mirror image and print it out for you.

MATERIALS

- Light-colored linen table runner, 14" x 90", with or without bead fringe at the ends
- Black-and-white images of floral basket, scroll, and cherub border (from *Decoupage: The Big Picture Sourcebook*, edited by Eleanor Hasbrouck Rawlings, Dover Publications)
- Black-and-white lettering to spell "ROSES" (from *Handbook of Renaissance Ornament: 1290*

Copyright-Free Designs for Artists and Craftsmen by Albert Fidelis Butsch, Dover Publications)

- 6 sheets of photo transfer paper
- 13 flat-backed crystal rhinestones, 5 mm
- 1 vial of black seed beads

Tools and Supplies

- Access to a photocopy machine or access to a computer, printer, scanner, and graphics software package
- Decoupage scissors
- Iron and ironing board
- Permanent beading glue
- Self-healing cutting mat
- Straightedge
- Tweezers
- X-Acto knife

⋟ Designer's Tips ⋞

- When using black-and-white engravings with the photo transfer process, choose a light-colored table runner made from a flat or tightly woven fabric for the best results.

- To ensure a straight border, transfer the border segments one at a time. Attempting to iron multiple pieces simultaneously will cause shifting and create a zigzag pattern instead of a straight line. To get great results, first position one piece on the runner, iron it on, and remove the backing. Then, when you position the second piece, check carefully to be sure that the patterns match up. Also, place a straightedge along the inside edge of the transferred border piece, extending the ruler to act as an alignment guide as you lay down the next piece.

Instructions

1. Iron the table runner to remove any wrinkles or folds, especially on the hemmed edges.

2. If using a photocopy machine to create the designs for the runner, see the Designer's Tip (right). If using a computer and scanner, scan the floral basket, scroll, letters, and border designs. Resize the images as desired. I enlarged the floral basket by about 200%, and I flipped the scroll upside down and enlarged it by about 350%. The letters were reduced by about 40%, and the border segment was reduced by about 60% so that it measured 1" wide and 10" long. Create one image by layering the scroll image over the basket and layering the letters over the scroll. Move the items around until the desired arrangement is achieved. Create a mirror image of the final design. Following the manufacturer's directions, print the design twice onto transfer paper. Copy the resized border to fit six on a page. Create a mirror image and print the borders onto transfer paper four times to make 24 border strips.

⋟ Designer's Tip ⋞

If you don't have access to a computer, printer, and scanner, photocopy the floral basket, scroll, letters, and border designs and resize them using the guidelines in step 2. Cut out the floral basket, scroll, and letters, and layer and arrange them on a clean sheet of paper as described in step 2. Secure the pieces in place with double-stick tape. Make a photocopy to test the design. Make adjustments if necessary. Following the manufacturer's directions, photocopy the final design twice onto photo transfer paper, using the mirror image setting on the copier. Photocopy the resized border six times and cut out. Tape the six borders to a clean sheet of paper. Photocopy the borders in reverse onto photo transfer paper four times to make 24 border strips.

3. Using decoupage scissors, trim away the excess paper around the floral basket designs on both printouts and set aside. On a self-healing cutting mat, cut out the borders using an X-Acto knife and straightedge ruler. Trim away the excess paper as close to the edges of the borders as possible and set aside.

4. Position the runner with one short end flat on your ironing board. Begin where the runner comes to a point. Place two border pieces face down, ⅛" from the outer edge of the runner, and unite the ends of the pieces at the point.

Where the border pieces meet, use the decoupage scissors to miter the corner to fit within the point.

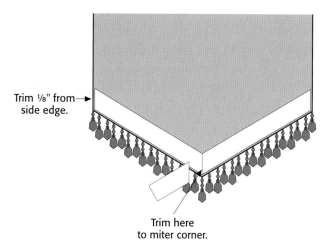

Trim ⅛" from side edge. →

Trim here to miter corner.

Remove the right border piece. Lay a third border piece, face down, ⅛" from the left edge of the long side of the runner. Lap the border piece from the pointed end over it. Trim the end of the side border piece so that the cut end butts against the top edge of the end border piece.

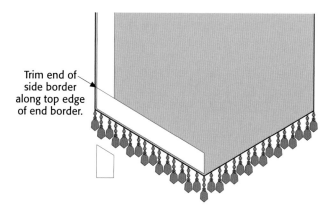

Trim end of side border along top edge of end border.

Repeat with a fourth border piece on the right edge of the runner. Set aside all border pieces except for one piece along the pointed end. Reposition this piece at the end of the runner, facedown. Following the manufacturer's direc-

tions, press the transfer design using a dry iron set on cotton or the highest setting. Run the iron over the entire border, paying close attention to all edges. Carefully lift off the paper backing. Transfer papers vary in terms of when to remove the backing paper (that is, when the image is still hot, or after it has cooled), so read the directions carefully. Position the remaining end border piece along the pointed end of the runner, face down. Be sure to line up the border pieces so the mitered corners and border patterns match. Transfer the design using the iron. Next transfer the remaining two border pieces, lining up the corners. Turn the runner to the opposite short side, smooth it flat on your ironing board, and repeat the border transfer process. Then apply the remaining border pieces to the entire length of both long sides of the runner in the same manner, ironing one border segment at a time and leaving no space in between.

5. Position the runner with one short end flat on the ironing board. Place the floral basket transfer face down and centered on the runner. Refer to the photo for placement. Following the manufacturer's directions, press the transfer with a hot iron. Run the iron over the entire image, paying close attention to all edges. Remove the backing paper to reveal the image. Turn the runner to the opposite short end and repeat to apply the second floral image.

6. Use tweezers and beading glue to apply flat-backed rhinestones over the floral basket design, referring to the project photo for placement. Next to each rhinestone, glue one black seed bead. Also glue one black seed bead at each corner of all block letters.

"La Vie En Rose" Pillow

By Genevieve A. Sterbenz

There are hard-working bed pillows that provide cozy support each night. And then, there are show pillows whose only purpose is to look beautiful. "La Vie En Rose" is the central theme of this decorative show pillow, used both literally and figuratively to express this romantic French idea.

Translated, "La Vie En Rose" means "Life is rosy." To emphasize the rose theme, accent rose-print fabric with embellishments in different shades of rose, from light pinks to reds, and stitch a dimensional silk rose to the pillow. A gold script "R" charm and embroidered branches with red berry clusters highlight the central panel, which features the phrase "La Vie En Rose" surrounded by pink seed beads. The central panel of this pillow is surrounded by beaded fringe and a border of a rich velvet animal print, adding texture and richness to the design.

Materials

- 16" square pillow form
- ½ yard of animal-print velvet
- ½ yard of rose-print upholstery cotton
- Matching thread
- 2 yards of amber beaded fringe, 1" long
- 2 yards of light green beaded ball fringe
- 1 artificial silk rose, approximately 4" in diameter with the stem removed
- 2 dozen chartreuse sequins
- 26 beaded berries, ⅜" wide
- 3 glass red beads, 5 mm wide
- Sequin roses: 5 sheer pink, 5 candy pink, 4 light pink, 3 moss green
- 1 vial of pink seed beads
- 1 skein of dark moss green embroidery floss
- 1 gold "R" charm with eyelet in script type, 1" high

TOOLS AND SUPPLIES

◆ Access to a color photocopy machine or access to a computer and color printer

◆ Embroidery scissors

◆ Fabri-Tac Permanent Adhesive (Beacon)

◆ Iron and ironing board

◆ Photo transfer paper

◆ Scissors

◆ Sewing and beading needles

◆ Sewing machine with size 12 or 14 needle

◆ Straight pins

◆ Straightedge

◆ Zipper foot attachment for sewing machine

⇒ DESIGNER'S TIP ⇐

If you can only find a silver letter charm, use a gold paint pen to transform it to gold.

INSTRUCTIONS

Note: The instructions below allow for ½" seam allowances.

1. For the center square of the pillow, measure and cut a 12½" square from rose-print fabric, selecting a portion of fabric with a pleasing array of blooms. Set the center square aside. For the borders, measure and cut four strips from the animal print, two measuring 3½" x 12½" and two measuring 3½" x 17½". Set the border strips aside. For the pillow backing, measure and cut a 17½" square from the animal print and set aside.

2. To make the "La Vie En Rose" message strip, measure and cut a 2" x 7¼" rectangle from a scrap of the rose print, selecting a pale area of the fabric. Turn and press ¼" hems on all sides. Photocopy the text on page 31 onto photo transfer paper, using the mirror-image

setting on the copier; or, using a computer, type the words "La Vie En Rose" using the Edwardian Script ITC font with a point size of 80 and a font color of pink. Print the words onto photo transfer paper in reverse, using a color printer. Use a ruler and scissors to measure and trim the message strip to 1½" x 6¾" so that the words are centered, eliminating all excess transfer paper. Set the iron to the cotton setting with no steam. Lay the fabric strip right side up on a protected work surface, unfold the hems, and smooth flat. Center the photo transfer strip right side down on the fabric. Use even, firm pressure to press over the paper. Follow the manufacturer's directions regarding the proper time to remove the paper backing. Refold the hems on the message strip. Center and pin the strip to the center floral square of fabric. Using a sewing machine, edgestitch around the message strip. Use a threaded beading needle to sew pink seed beads around the edges of the message strip, spacing the beads about ⅛" apart.

3. Use a pencil to lightly draw floral stems over the center fabric square. Use the floral pattern in the fabric as a guide for the direction in which to draw the stems. In the project shown, most of the stems were drawn projecting out from the message strip. See the collage plan on page 31. If your floral fabric has stems, you can use them instead. Create as many or as few as desired. Outline the drawn stems using a stem stitch with an embroidery needle threaded with six strands of moss green embroidery floss.

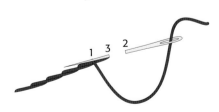

Stem Stitch

4. Use a sewing needle threaded with one strand of floss to sew sequins to the center square in a random pattern. Use the collage plan on page 31 and the project photo as guides for placement. Use a threaded sewing needle to tack beaded berries to the embroidered stems and to attach the sequin roses. Also add dabs of glue to the undersides of the sequin roses, if necessary. Use a sewing needle to tack the silk rose and script "R" charm to the center square, referring to the project photo and collage plan for placement.

5. Lay the center square right side up on a flat surface. Pin and hand baste the amber beaded fringe around all four sides, with the fringe facing the center of the panel. Clip into the fringe heading at the corners, if necessary, for it to lie flat. Pin and hand baste the beaded ball fringe over the beaded amber fringe; clip the fringe heading at the corners, if necessary. Attach a zipper foot to your sewing machine and stitch the layered fringes to the sides of the center square, being careful not to sew over the beads.

Stitch both layers of fringe to the center square
along the inner edge of the fringe heading.
Clip fringe heading at corners.

6. Lay the center square right side up on a flat surface. Pin the shorter animal-print strips to the sides of the center square, making certain that the beaded fringe is hanging away from the seam allowances. Machine stitch with a zipper foot ½" from the raw edges on both sides. Lay the pillow front right side up on a flat surface. Pin the longer animal-print strips to the top and bottom edges of the pillow front and stitch ½" from the raw edges, being careful not to catch the fringe in the seams.

7. To finish the pillow, lay the pillow front on a flat surface, right side up. Center the pillow back, right side down, on the pillow front. Align the outer edges and pin. Machine stitch ½" from the raw edges, leaving an opening for turning. Trim the corners diagonally ⅛" from the stitching. Turn the pillow cover to the right side. Compress the pillow form and insert it into the opening. Use a threaded sewing needle to slip-stitch the opening closed.

Collage Plan

La Vie En Rose

Cabbage Rose
Charger Plate and Napkin Ring

By Genevieve A. Sterbenz

Simple cutting and gluing transforms a plain gold charger plate into an elegant show-piece for your table. The cabbage rose images and coordinating papers were selected from a set of Anna Griffin decoupage papers. Crystal rhinestone accents were added for a subtle sparkle. For the matching napkin ring, start with a store-bought gold ring that is wide and smooth to make it easy to cover the ring with the paper images. Complete the ring with a gold filigree jewelry accent and a crystal rhinestone centered on top.

Materials
(FOR ONE CHARGER
AND ONE NAPKIN RING)

- 13" gold charger plate
- 1½"-wide gold napkin ring, 2" in diameter
- 3 packages of Royal Coat Decoupage Paper Packs in the Anna Griffin Cabbage Roses design (Plaid item #2068)
- Decoupage glue in glossy finish
- 1 flat gold filigree jewelry accent, 1.5 cm
- 19 flat-backed crystal rhinestones, 5 mm
- Gold paint pen
- Permanent beading glue

Tools and Supplies

- Compass
- Decoupage scissors
- Glass cleaner
- Paper towels
- Self-healing cutting mat
- Sponge brush
- Straightedge
- Tweezers
- X-Acto knife

When applying the larger center circles of paper, be sure to smooth away any air bubbles or wrinkles as best you can. Still, the paper will most likely buckle. Do not be too concerned, as the paper will smooth out some when the glue dries completely.

INSTRUCTIONS (FOR CHARGER)

1. Cut out 19 cabbage rose groupings from the paper packs, using the decoupage scissors and eliminating small rose buds, if desired. Set aside. From the same pages, cut out 18 small pale pink flowers with blue centers from the garlands and set aside. Using the X-Acto knife and self-healing cutting mat, measure, mark, and cut nine 1½" squares from green floral paper and set aside. Measure, mark, and cut nine 3¼"-long light pink stripes with ⅛" dark pink borders from the pink striped paper and set aside. Using a compass, measure and mark a 7"-diameter circle on the pink striped paper. Cut out and set aside. Also measure, mark, and cut circles 7½" and 8" in diameter from green floral paper. On the smaller green circle, measure, center, and mark a 6¾"-diameter circle. Cut out the inner circle and discard it, leaving a ⅜" border. Set aside. On the larger green circle, measure, center, and mark a 7¼"-diameter circle, and then cut it out and discard, leaving a ⅜" border. Set aside.

2. Clean the charger thoroughly with glass cleaner to remove all dust and fingerprints. Using a sponge brush, apply a light coat of decoupage glue to the back of one pink stripe. Position the stripe on the charger as shown. One end should cover the outside rim of the charger and the opposite end should overlap

the inner circle of the plate slightly. Smooth away any air bubbles with your hands. Position the remaining eight pink stripes, without glue, at equidistant spaces around the charger. Measuring along the inner rim of the charger, they should be about 1¾" apart. Once in position, glue them down.

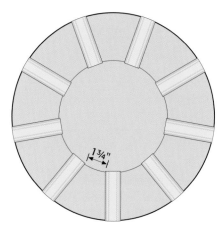

Glue pink stripes to rim of charger.

3. Center and glue one green floral square over one stripe in a diamond position. Repeat with the remaining squares. Position and glue one cabbage rose grouping over each green square, with roses pointing away from the center of the plate.

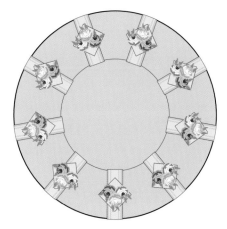

Glue green squares and cabbage rose groupings to the center of each stripe.

4. Position and glue nine of the remaining cabbage rose groupings between the stripes along the outer rim of the charger, with the roses pointing toward the center of the plate. Position and glue two pale pink flowers with blue centers on each side of one stripe at the outer rim of the charger. Repeat for the remaining stripes.

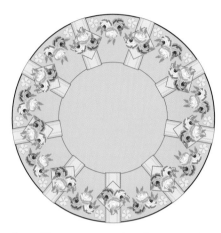

Glue cabbage rose groupings between stripes, and glue pale pink and blue flowers along sides of stripes near outer edge.

5. Position and glue the larger green border circle around the inner rim of the plate. The paper may wrinkle slightly, so press and smooth down as much as possible. Repeat with the smaller green border circle so that it overlaps the inner edge of the first border circle. Position and glue the pink striped circle in the center of the charger, overlapping the edge of the green border circle. Position and glue the remaining cabbage rose grouping to the center of the charger.

6. Using a sponge brush, apply a light coat of decoupage glue over the entire top surface of the plate and let dry.

7. Apply one rhinestone to the center of each pale pink flower with blue center, using tweezers and beading glue. Let dry. Use the gold paint pen to draw a circle around the outside of the pink striped center circle.

INSTRUCTIONS (FOR NAPKIN RING)

1. Using decoupage scissors, cut out four large coordinating floral clusters from the same paper sheets as the cabbage roses. Apply a light coat of decoupage glue to the back of one floral cluster. Center over the napkin ring and press to adhere. Any overlap should be wrapped around the top and bottom edges of the ring and adhered to the inside. Repeat with the remaining three floral clusters until the napkin ring is completely covered.

2. On the self-healing cutting mat, use the X-Acto knife to cut out a light pink stripe, 8" long. Apply glue to the back of the stripe and wrap it around the center of the napkin ring. Where the ends meet, overlap slightly and trim away the excess. Use beading glue to apply the gold filigree jewelry accent to the center top of the napkin ring over the pink stripe. Glue a rhinestone to the center of the gold jewelry accent.

FRENCH MEMO BOARD

By Saralyn Ewald, Creative Coordinator, Archiver's: The Photo Memory Store

If you're looking for a place to keep track of notes, to-do lists, invitations, and more, make this stylish ribbon board to keep things neatly in order. A corkboard was covered with torn pieces of script paper and then woven with ribbons, allowing you to trap cards under the ribbons as well as pin items in place. Use a variety of black and white ribbons. At the ribbon intersections, add ribbon charms and buttons for embellishment.

MATERIALS

- 11" x 14" wall frame (Interior Accents Collection)
- 2 pieces of 11" x 14" rolled cork (Quartet)
- 3 sheets of 12" x 12" paper for background (script and buttons printed flat paper by K and Company)
- 14" length of striped ribbon ("Paris Chic" Embellishment Kit by Westrim Crafts)
- "Avenue Des Champs-Élysées" ribbon (#4904 by Mokuba) cut to the following lengths:
  - 1 piece, 15"
  - 1 piece, 16"
- White ribbon with music notes and lyrics (#4898 by Mokuba) cut to the following lengths:
  - 1 piece, 20"
  - 1 piece, 8"

- Black ribbon with music notes (#4899 by Mokuba) cut to the following lengths:
  - 1 piece, 11½"
  - 1 piece, 13"
  - 1 piece, 9"
  - 3 pieces, 1½"
- "Boulevard Montmartre" ribbon (#4900 by Mokuba) cut to the following lengths:
  - 1 piece, 19"
  - 1 piece, 1½"
- 5 ribbon charms (Making Memories Rectangle Variety Pack)
- 5 assorted antique white or black buttons, at least 1" in diameter
- Super 77 Spray Adhesive (3M)
- Wonder Tape roll, ⅜" width (Suze Weinberg)
- Wonder Tape sheets, four ½" x ¾" pieces (Suze Weinberg)

Tools and Supplies

- ◆ Duct tape (3M)
- ◆ Heavy books
- ◆ Kraft paper
- ◆ Scissors
- ◆ Self-healing cutting mat
- ◆ Wax paper
- ◆ X-Acto knife

Instructions

1. Disassemble the frame, carefully removing the backboard and glass. You will not need the glass. Cover your work surface with kraft paper and position the backboard on the kraft paper. Spray the front of the backboard with spray adhesive, covering the whole surface without saturating it.

2. Press one piece of cork over the glued surface, carefully lining up the cork to cover the entire board surface. Apply pressure as you smooth down the surface of the cork. Place the board, cork side down, on a smooth, even surface. (You may want to cover the surface with wax paper to protect it from excess glue.) Stack heavy books on top of the upside-down cork to apply pressure as it dries (approximately 10 to 15 minutes).

3. Once dry, place the board, cork side down, on a self-healing cutting mat and use an X-Acto knife to trim off the excess cork so that it is flush with the board.

4. Glue and trim the second piece of cork to the first cork surface in the same manner.

5. Tear the three sheets of paper for background into asymmetrical pieces no smaller than 2" x 2" and no larger than 4" x 4". Working with one piece at a time, lightly spray the back of a piece of torn paper and attach it to the cork surface. Continue adhering the pieces of torn paper to the cork surface at various angles, overlapping them until the whole surface is covered. Place the board, paper side down, on

a cutting mat and trim off the excess paper with an X-Acto knife.

6. Position the 11½" length of black ribbon with music notes at the top right corner of the paper-covered surface, 5" to the left of the corner at the top edge and 6" down from the corner on the right edge. Keeping the ribbon taut, tape each end to the back of the board with a small piece of duct tape.

7. Slide a metal ribbon charm onto the 14" length of striped ribbon, stopping in the center. Leaving about 2¾" of space from the previously secured ribbon, position the striped ribbon parallel to the music note ribbon. It is very important for the ribbons to be perfectly parallel. Keep the ribbon tight as you secure it to the back of the board with duct tape.

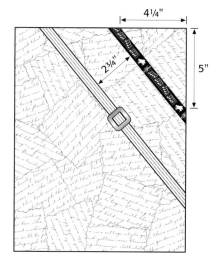

8. Position the 20" length of white ribbon with music notes and lyrics about 2¾" from the secured striped ribbon, keeping the ribbons perfectly parallel. Secure tightly to the back of the board with duct tape.

9. Position the 13" length of black ribbon with music notes about 2¾" from the secured white ribbon, keeping the ribbons perfectly parallel. Secure tightly to the back of the board with duct tape.

10. In the top left corner, place the 8" length of white ribbon with music notes and lyrics. Gently slide one end of the ribbon under the

secured striped ribbon. Wrap the right end of the ribbon to the back of the board, 2" to the right of the corner at the top edge, and secure with duct tape. Wrap the left end to the back, 2" below the corner on the left edge, and secure tightly on the back with duct tape.

11. Position the 15" length of "Avenue Des Champs-Élysées" ribbon about 2¾" from the secured white ribbon with musical notes, keeping the ribbons perfectly parallel. Slide one end under the perpendicular secured white ribbon, over the striped ribbon and under the black music ribbon. Attach the ends of the ribbon to the back of the board securely with duct tape.

12. Position the 19" length of "Boulevard Montmartre" ribbon about 2¾" from the "Avenue Des Champs-Élysées" ribbon, keeping the ribbons parallel. Slide one end of the ribbon under the lower piece of black music note ribbon, over the white music note ribbon, under the ribbon charm on the striped ribbon, and over the upper black music note ribbon. Pull the ribbon taught and secure on the back with duct tape.

13. Position the 16" length of "Avenue Des Champs-Élysées" ribbon about 2¾" from the "Boulevard Montmartre" ribbon, keeping the ribbons parallel. Starting at the bottom, carefully slide the ribbon over the black music note ribbon, under the white music note ribbon, over the striped ribbon, and under the black music note ribbon. Use duct tape to secure the two ends of the ribbon to the back of the board.

14. Position the 9" length of black ribbon with music notes in the lower right corner, about 2¾" from the "Avenue Des Champs-Élysées" ribbon, keeping the ribbons parallel. The ribbon can overlap the other ribbons it crosses. Secure the ends on the back with duct tape. Review the placement of the ribbons and make adjustments to fine-tune their placement, if desired.

15. Thread a small piece of black ribbon with music notes through one of the ribbon charms and secure the two ends to the back of the charm with a small piece of duct tape. Make sure the ends are as flat as possible. Repeat with the remaining ribbon charms, threading two with the black ribbon and one with a short piece of "Boulevard Montmartre" ribbon.

16. Apply a ½" x ¾" piece of Wonder Tape to the back of each of the ribbon charms. Peel the protective backing from the tape and adhere each ribbon charm as follows (use the project photo on page 36 as a guide, if necessary): one charm with black ribbon at each of the two intersections of the black music note ribbon and the "Boulevard Montmartre" ribbon; the charm with white ribbon at the intersection of the "Boulevard Montmartre" ribbon and the white music note ribbon; and the last charm with black ribbon at the intersection of the black music note ribbon and the white music note ribbon.

17. Insert the memo board into the wooden frame. The thickness of the two layers of cork will take up the space previously filled by the glass.

18. Attach an antique button at each of the remaining ribbon intersections, using a small piece of Wonder Tape. Alternate between white and black buttons if possible.

≥ DESIGNER'S TIP ≤

You can tuck cards and memos into the ribbons to hold them in place or use white-headed stickpins to secure memorabilia to the board. If using pins, stick them into the printed portion of the ribbons to hide any puncture holes that otherwise might show on the paper. For added embellishment, slide Paris-inspired charms onto the pins before sticking them to the board.

Mosaic Candle Luminary

By Jill MacKay

This mosaic candle luminary will add a touch of whimsy to any environment. The mosaic design is a pleasure to look at, and with its encouraging words, it's sure to be noticed and admired by friends and family alike. The flickering candlelight will cast an interesting glow through the sparkling shards of glass, adding warmth to any room or table setting.

This project is created with several kinds of glass. Clear glass shards and clear glass gems are used over the areas with words, so the text can easily be seen through the glass. Textured clear glass is also used. "Ring mottle" stained glass is a style of stained glass first popularized by Tiffany. It features a mixture of colors that create ring-like effects throughout the glass. Pink and amber were used for this project. "Streaky" stained glass is a style in which rich colors are draped or appear to streak across the sheet of glass. A piece with pink, amber, and ruby tones was used here. A piece of stained glass in a transparent ruby hue was used to create wavy dividing lines between the areas of clear and variegated glass. The words seen through the clear glass are photocopied onto a sheet of decal paper that can be cut to size and adhered directly to the glass.

MATERIALS

- Glass pedestal vase, 7½" diameter x 11¾" tall
- 7" x 12" sheet of ring mottle stained glass (pinks and ambers)
- 7" x 12" piece of streaky stained glass (pinks, ambers, and ruby)
- 6" x 12" piece of dark ruby translucent stained glass
- 4" x 4" piece of dark green stained glass
- 6" x 12" piece of double-thickness lightly textured clear glass
- 3" x 12" piece of double-thickness heavily textured clear glass
- 7 small clear glass gems with flat backs (available in packages of 25 mosaic marbles by Plaid)
- 8½" x 11" sheet of Lazertran waterslide decal paper (regular)
- 2-oz. bottle of liquid pure pigment in red (Createx)
- 1-lb. carton of white sanded grout (plaid)
- 4-oz. tube of clear silicone adhesive

Note: Most stained glass is sold in sheets 12" x 12" or larger. The sizes listed here are the actual amounts of glass used in this project. The exact amount needed is listed for those who may already have a scrap box of stained glass so that they can determine whether they'll need to purchase more glass to complete this project.

TOOLS AND SUPPLIES

- Access to a computer and printer (optional)
- Access to a color photocopy machine
- Black permanent marker
- Breaking pliers
- Craft sticks
- 2 disposable containers or small buckets (for grouting)
- Dust mask
- Glass cleaner
- Glass cutters
- Heat gun
- Mosaic glass cutters (Plaid)
- Paper towels
- Plastic (to cover work surface)
- Polishing cloth (soft material, such as an old T-shirt, not terry cloth)
- Razor blade
- Rubber gloves
- Ruler
- Safety glasses
- Scissors
- Sponge
- Toothpicks
- Old towel (to rest the vase on)

⇒ DESIGNER'S TIPS ⇐

- Always wear safety goggles while cutting or nipping glass.

- You will find that fitting odd-shaped pieces together gets easier and easier. The more you do it, the more you will develop an "eye" for it. You'll learn to spot the shape you need, and the amount of extra nipping and refining you do will decrease. It's like putting a puzzle together, looking for the piece that's just the right shape.

- Draw the pattern design on the inside of the vase so you can easily clean away the lines once you have finished the piece.

- When gluing, spread the glue around on the surface of the vase with the nozzle tip of the glue tube. Make sure there is enough glue to securely adhere the piece of stained glass to the surface, but not so much that when you press it firmly in place the glue squishes up and fills the spaces between pieces. These spaces are for the grout. Use a craft stick to clear away any extra glue that has oozed out. The spaces between pieces should be approximately 1/16" wide or slightly larger, and should be fairly consistent throughout the project.

- When gluing clear glass, you must be extra careful because the glue will show to a much greater extent. If you don't press hard enough you will not squeeze out all the air bubbles. If you have not applied enough glue to the surface of the vase before you press a piece of glass down, the spaces where there is a lack of glue will be even more noticeable than air bubbles. So work carefully while positioning with the clear glass shards. You will not be able to avoid all of the air bubbles, but do your best.

INSTRUCTIONS

1. There is no pattern included with this project, as it consists simply of four wavy lines. Using the permanent marker, place your hand inside the vase and, approximately 2" up from the bottom of the vase, draw a gently waving line forming a complete circle around the interior of the vase. Move up approximately 1¼" and draw the second wavy line. Next, move up 2¼" and draw the third wavy line. Measure up another 2½" and draw the top, final wavy line.

2. Photocopy the words on page 46 in color onto the Lazertran paper, following the manufacturer's instructions and using the mirror-image setting on a color copier. Or, using a computer and word-processing program, type the words "DREAM," "HOPE," and "LOVE," in capital letters, using the Algerian font in 72-point size and leaving a space between each letter. Then change the font size to 10 points and type the words "LAUGH," "GIVE," "CARE," "LUCK," "WISH," "JOY," and "LIVE." You do not need to leave spaces between the letters this time, but do leave several spaces between each word. Make sure that these words will fit in their entirety under the glass gems where they will be placed. Set the font color for brown. Using the mirror-image or reverse function in your word processor or printer, print the text onto paper in reverse. If you're unable to print the text in reverse, you can print the text as you normally would and then take the paper to a photocopy center to have it copied in reverse. Photocopy the words in color onto the Lazertran paper, following the manufacturer's instructions.

3. Use your scissors to cut out the large words. Cut out each letter separately, and leave enough space around the characters so that their overall size after cutting is approximately a 1" x 1¼" rectangle. Following the manufacturer's instructions for the decal paper, adhere

the three large words in the space between the upper two wavy lines. Position each of the letters at a slightly different angle to give them a whimsical appearance, almost as if they are dancing or floating. Leave an equal amount of space between the letters of each word, and a slightly greater amount of space between the words. Cut out the smaller words into ovals and slide each word onto the flat bottom of a glass gem, making sure that if you turn the gem over and look down into it you can read the word. It will feel like the decals do not adhere as well to the glass gems. Do not worry, just get them in the right place and leave them to dry with the flat side up. Let the vase and the glass gems dry overnight. The next day, heat the decals lightly with a heat gun to make the Lazertran letters become more permanently affixed as well as clearer to look at. This doesn't take long. Watch each letter carefully and don't overdo it; overheated decals shrivel, turn black, and burn up.

4. Using the silicone adhesive, glue the glass gems onto the vase, placing them in the dips above the uppermost wavy line and in the rises below the second wavy line. (Refer to the collage plan on page 45 and to the project photo for placement.) Let dry.

5. Using the glass cutters and a ruler, score and cut the dark ruby translucent stained glass into strips approximately $5/16$" wide, running the length of the sheet of glass. Try to keep your strips as uniform in size as possible. After scoring and cutting all of the ruby glass into strips, use the mosaic glass cutters and nip the strips into smaller squares and rectangles ranging from $1/4$" to $3/8$" long. You don't have to be too careful about the sizing here.

6. Carefully lay the vase on its side on an old towel, making sure that it will not roll off. Begin by gluing the small ruby squares onto the wavy lines. Work on all four lines on the

section of the vase that is facing upward. Then turn the vase until the next empty section is facing you, and continue gluing and turning the vase until you have completed all of the wavy lines. Make sure that you allow the glue on each section to dry sufficiently before you place that section down on the towel, otherwise the glass pieces may become dislodged. Pay close attention to keeping a uniform amount of space between each piece of glass. Once you have finished all the wavy lines on the body of the vase, carefully stand the vase upright and glue two lines of ruby stained glass at the base—one ring on the inside edge and one ring along the outside edge.

7. Using the mosaic glass cutters, nip the ring mottle stained glass and the streaky stained glass into randomly shaped shards. Let these shards mix together as you desire. Some may need to be reshaped for a perfect fit, and some will be just the right shape as they are. Glue these shards to the foot of the vase, nipping to shape when necessary. Next, carefully lay the vase back down on its side on the towel. To glue the shards in place on the body of the vase, you will once again be working in one upturned section at a time. Fill in the three pink sections of the body as marked on the collage plan. Note that in the section at the base of the vase, where there is greater curvature, you will need to nip the shards into smaller pieces in order for them to lie flat. Whenever you place a glass shard on a surface and it rocks back and forth, it is too large and will not adhere properly. Simply remove the piece and nip it to a smaller size so it lies perfectly flat.

8. Using the mosaic glass cutters, nip the heavily textured clear glass into randomly shaped shards. Working your way around the vase, use these pieces to fill the space between the two lower wavy lines.

9. Using the mosaic glass cutters, nip the lightly textured clear glass into randomly shaped shards. Glue the shards to the last open section. Pay particular attention when gluing over the letters so that most of the text is covered with glass, not left open, since the open space between pieces will be filled with grout and will obstruct the view of the letter. You can even place the glass shards a little closer together than elsewhere to ensure clear viewing of the letter once the piece is grouted. Fill in this entire section. Let dry overnight.

10. Clear away all glass shards and other materials, and cover your work surface with plastic in preparation to grout. Next, clean the entire surface of the vase, using a craft stick or razor blade to scrape off any residual glue from the surface of the glass.

Collage Plan

▨ Pink mix

☐ Lightly textured clear

▤ Heavily textured clear

■ Ruby red

11. Put on the dust mask. Pour the grout into one container and fill the other with water. Add two drops of red pure pigment to the dry grout. Following the manufacturer's instructions, add water and mix the grout thoroughly until it is an even color and is the consistency of thick oatmeal. If you want to make the color more intense, simply add another drop of pigment. Apply the grout over the entire surface of the vase, both the body and the base. Using gloved fingertips, firmly press the grout down into the crevices. Along the outside edge on the base and the upper rim of the vase you will want to carefully smooth these grout lines with your fingertips.

12. Wet the sponge in water, wringing out the excess. Begin to clean by sponging away the excess grout, but be careful not to sponge away too much grout. You may need to go back and fix the grout lines along the top and bottom edges if small amounts of the grout became dislodged by the sponge. Just add a little more grout with your fingertips and smooth again. Let dry 10 to 15 minutes. Polish clean with a soft cloth. You may need to go over the heavily textured clear glass section with a craft stick or toothpick to clean some stubborn spots, as the heavy texture will hold extra grout.

13. Spray the inside of the vase with glass cleaner and wipe away the marker lines with a paper towel.

DREAM

HOPE

LOVE

LAUGH

GIVE

CARE

LUCK

WISH

JOY

LIVE

LA CUCINA CLOCK

By Genevieve A. Sterbenz

Customizing a clock to match any decor is so simple when you start with a plain wood base and precut wallpaper images. Wooden clock bases, clock movement mechanisms, and adhesive numerals are very easy to work with and are available at most craft stores.

A number of different techniques and materials were used to create this clock. The face of the clock is covered with wallpaper cutouts and the numerals are placed within a rubber-stamped block consisting of a pear inside a border. The outer rim of the clock is painted sage green and rubbed with gold wax for an antique look. A fine gold trim is added between the painted border and the face of the clock. And finally, metal letters spell out the words *La Cucina* (Italian for *kitchen*) on the face of the clock.

MATERIALS

- Round wooden clock base (Walnut Hollow #23026, extra large)
- Quartz clock movement (Walnut Hollow #TQ710)
- Gold clock hands (Walnut Hollow #1006)
- Gold ⅝" Arabic numerals (Walnut Hollow #592)
- 1 package of the Susan Winget Fruit pattern of Wallies Wallpaper Cutouts (#12974)
- 1 package of the Tapestry Cutouts pattern from the Trading Spaces collection of Wallies Wallpaper Cutouts (#12999)
- 4 packages of the Love Letters Mural pattern from the Trading Spaces collection of Wallies Wallpaper Cutouts (#13448)

- 1" eyelet script letters to spell "La Cucina" (Making Memories)
- 1 yard of gold rope trim
- White primer
- Sage green acrylic paint
- Gold leaf metallic wax finish (Rub N Buff)
- 1⅛"-square rubber stamp with pear image and border (Brenda Walton's Tuscan Garden Rubber Stamp Set from All Night Media by Plaid)
- Gold dye ink pad
- Gold paint pen
- Clear-drying permanent glue (Fabric-Tac Permanent Adhesive by Beacon)

Tools and Supplies

◆ Craft scissors

◆ Decoupage scissors

◆ Kraft paper

◆ Newspaper

◆ Soft cotton cloth

◆ Sponge brush, 1"-wide

◆ Spray adhesive

◆ Ruler

◆ Tweezers

Instructions

1. Cover a clean, flat work surface with kraft paper. Using the sponge brush, apply two light coats of primer to the clock, allowing the paint to dry between coats. Apply two coats of sage green paint to the clock, allowing the paint to dry between coats. Place a small amount of gold leaf finish on a cotton cloth and rub it into the cloth. Rub the cloth over the outer rim of the clock to apply gold accents over the green painted surface. Let dry.

2. Remove the Italian text cutouts from the Love Letters Mural packages of Wallies. There will be two in each package for a total of eight; set two aside. Position six of the cutouts on the clock face, overlapping them, until the entire face is covered. The cutouts will extend beyond the edges of the clock face and will be trimmed later. Pick up one cutout at a time and place it face down on a second work surface covered with clean newspaper. Apply a light coat of spray adhesive. Turn the cutout to the right side and place it back in position on the clock face, smoothing flat with your hands. Repeat with the remaining pieces until covered. Using the decoupage scissors, trim away the excess around the edge of the clock face and set aside the scraps. With your finger, find the hole in the center of the clock. Cut an X over the hole using the decoupage scissors and trim away the cutouts covering the hole.

3. Referring to the project photo for placement, position two pear cutouts from the Susan Winget Fruit package of Wallies and one floral cutout from the Tapestry Floral Cutouts package in the center of the clock face. The images should slightly overlap to create bottom, middle, and top cutout layers. Remove the bottom cutout first and place face down on clean newspaper. Apply a thin coat of spray adhesive, and then return the cutout to the original position on the clock face, pressing down to adhere. Repeat with the middle and top layers to form the center collage. Locate the center hole and trim away excess paper using decoupage scissors as before.

4. With the rubber stamp and gold ink, create 12 stamped images on the Italian text wallpaper cutouts that you set aside earlier. Cut out and position the images around the clock face. Use a ruler to establish equal quadrants and spaces between them. Remove the stamped squares one at a time and apply a light coat of spray adhesive to the back. Replace each square in its original position and smooth flat with your hands to adhere. With craft scissors, cut the clock numerals from the plastic casing. Remove the adhesive backing and position the numerals over the stamped squares on the clock face.

5. Using craft scissors, trim away the eyelets from the script letters. Place the letters face up on kraft paper. Use the gold paint pen to change the letters from silver to gold, and let dry. Using glue and tweezers, position and adhere the letters in place on the face of the clock, using the project photo on page 48 as a guide for placement.

6. Apply a small dab of glue on the side edge of the clock face. Position and press one end of the gold trim on the glue. Continue adding dabs of glue and pressing the trim in place around the clock face. Cut the trim where the ends meet.

7. Following the manufacturer's directions, assemble and add the quartz movement and hands to the clock.

"LET THEM EAT CAKE" CAKE PLATE AND DOME

By Genevieve A. Sterbenz

Glass etching, painting, and decoupage all contribute to the whimsical look of this cake plate. It is so much fun that you may just find yourself serving cake a lot more often.

The rich layered look is achieved by embellishing both the underside and the serving side of the plate. The majority of the etching, painting, and decoupage are applied on the underside, while the small polka dot details and the writing are done on the serving side and are permanent, so they will hold up to frequent use. The paper cutouts used were Wallies Wallpaper Cutouts, which work especially well here because they are sturdy and vinyl coated. If you choose not to use Wallies Wallpaper Cutouts, be careful to use a similar sturdy vinyl image. Simple gift wrap or fine specialty paper will not likely hold up during the etching process.

⇒ DESIGNER'S TIP ⇐

Although air-dry permanent glass and ceramic paints are available, most of them come with a warning: Painted surfaces should never come in contact with food. So be sure to check all labels when buying paint. Pēbēo Porcelaine 150 Paints were used for this project. They are easy to work with, safe for use with food items, become permanent when baked, and brushes can be cleaned with water. The manufacturer's directions advise that you wait at least 24 hours before baking, but if you applied several coats of paint, I advise waiting no less than 48 hours, and longer if you can. Paint that has not dried thoroughly will bubble when baked, making the design (and bubbles) permanent. Although baking the paint makes the cake plate dishwasher safe, careful hand washing is recommended so as not to risk ruining the cutouts.

MATERIALS

- Footed glass cake plate with dome
- 2 packages of the Tracy Porter Fruits and Flowers pattern of Wallies Wallpaper Cutouts (#12991)
- Etching cream
- Pēbēo Porcelaine 150 Paint in the following colors: Topaz, Malachite, Ivory, Peridot, and Anthracite Black
- Pēbēo Porcelaine 150 Outliner in Tourmaline and Marseille Yellow
- Light pink acrylic paint
- Mod Podge, gloss

TOOLS AND SUPPLIES

- Cotton swabs
- Disposable plastic plates
- Foam brush
- Glass cleaner
- Glass cup or dish of water
- Kraft paper
- Masking tape, ⅛" and ½" widths
- Newspaper
- Paintbrushes: one very fine for thin lines and one flat, ⅜" wide
- Paper towels
- Pencil
- Plastic drop cloth
- Pointy-end tweezers
- Rubber gloves
- Rubbing alcohol
- Scissors
- Spray adhesive
- Straightedge
- Tape measure

INSTRUCTIONS (FOR CAKE PLATE)

1. Cover a clean, flat work surface with kraft paper, a second work surface with newspaper, and a third with a drop cloth. Clean the cake plate thoroughly using glass cleaner and paper towels to remove all grease, dust, and fingerprints. Place the cake plate footed side up on the kraft paper. Wrap the tape measure around the roll of ½"-wide masking tape and make tick marks with a pencil every ½". Then, use scissors to cut the tape at each tick mark, creating ½" squares. Starting at the outside edge of the plate on the underside and working toward the center, use tweezers to lay down the squares of tape in a checkerboard pattern. It will be necessary to continue cutting tape squares until there are enough for three checkerboard rows around the outside of the plate. Use the back of the tweezers or a gloved hand to smooth down the tape squares, ensuring that all edges are sealed. If a corner lifts up, replace with a new square of tape. This prevents the etching cream from seeping underneath and altering the checkerboard design. To protect the top edge and serving side of the plate, run a length of ½"-wide masking tape around the outer edge of the plate on the underside, so that one edge of the tape touches the edge of the first row of taped squares. Fold the excess tape over onto the front of the plate. Still working on the back of the plate, run a length of ⅛"-wide masking tape inside the inner checkerboard row to form a circle, overlapping the tape where the ends meet. This is the row closest to the center of the plate. The tape should touch the edges of the taped squares. Narrow masking tape is easier to negotiate around curves and will provide cleaner lines and more concentric circles. Next, following that circle, lay down a circle of ½"-wide masking tape against it, making small tucks as necessary. Lay down

another circle of ⅛"-wide masking tape along the inside edge of the ½"-wide tape so that it is bordered on both sides.

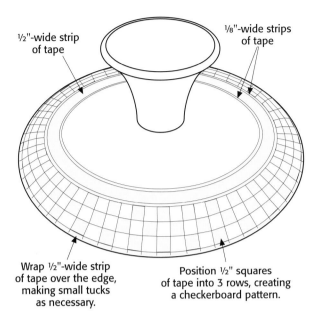

½"-wide strip of tape

⅛"-wide strips of tape

Wrap ½"-wide strip of tape over the edge, making small tucks as necessary.

Position ½" squares of tape into 3 rows, creating a checkerboard pattern.

2. Remove five strawberry cutouts from the packages of Wallies Wallpaper Cutouts. Position them, face down, around the taped circle so that the top edges rest on the second row of the checkerboard pattern. Leave about 1" spaces between the outermost leaves on the cutouts. When in place, secure with a small piece of masking tape. Use the adhesive dots provided in the Wallies package to mark the position of the cutouts. Remove one of the cutouts and place it face up on the newspaper-covered work surface. Apply spray adhesive. Lift the cutout off the newspaper with tweezers and replace it, face down, in position on the cake plate. Smooth flat with your hand, making sure all the edges are flush with the glass. Again, this is important to prevent the etching cream from seeping under the cutouts. Repeat with the remaining cutouts. Remove the extra pieces of masking tape and adhesive dots. To create the center stripes, run lengths of ½"-wide masking tape from the center of the plate to the taped circle. Begin by taping an X to create equal quadrants. The tape ends at the center of the plate should

move up and onto the foot. The opposite ends of the tape should either overlap the cutouts or end at the taped circle. Using the same technique, create three more stripes, all equal distances apart, within one quadrant. Repeat adding stripes to the remaining three quadrants. Run a length of tape around the foot where it meets the plate to prevent getting etching cream on the foot. Check the edges of all the taped areas and make sure they are flush with the glass. Use a small amount of glass cleaner on a cotton swab to remove stray fingerprints on the exposed areas of the glass. Do not soak the swab or it may loosen the tape. To etch the plate, place the cake plate, taped side up, on a drop cloth. Put on rubber gloves. Using a foam brush, follow the manufacturer's directions and apply etching cream to the back of the plate only. Do not apply etching cream to the foot of the plate. Use a patting motion to apply the cream. Avoid sweeping side-to-side strokes, as they will increase the chances of seepage. After five minutes, rinse the plate with water until all the cream is removed. Use a gloved hand to rub away the excess cream. Some tape and cutouts will rub off during the rinsing process. When all the cream is removed, remove the tape and the cutouts too. Dry off the plate and use cotton swabs and rubbing alcohol to remove stray beads of spray adhesive that have been left behind.

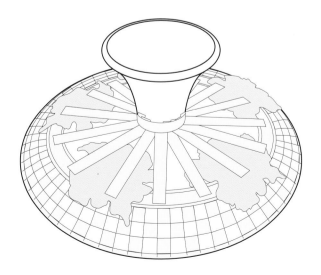

3. Place the cake plate, footed side up, on a work surface covered with kraft paper. Apply ½"-wide masking tape around the foot where it meets the plate to protect it. Take five more strawberry cutouts from the packages of Wallies Wallpaper Cutouts. Apply spray adhesive to the front of the cutouts and, one at a time, place them exactly as they were in the non-etched areas of the plate, lining up all the edges. Press the cutouts down so they are flush with the glass. On a plastic plate, pour out equal amounts of Topaz and Ivory paints and mix together, creating pink. Lay a straightedge along one stripe. Paint the stripe with pink paint, using the straightedge to help achieve a clean line. Lift off the straightedge, clean with a damp paper towel, and move it to the opposite edge on the stripe. Apply paint again until the entire stripe is covered, painting up to, but not into the non-etched circle near the outer edge. Don't worry about painting onto the back of the cutouts, but turn the plate over to make sure paint hasn't seeped between the cutouts and the glass. Repeat the process to paint all the center stripes pink, applying several coats to ensure even coverage. Let dry. Next, mix three parts Malachite paint with one part Ivory paint on a separate plastic plate to create light green. Paint the circle border on the non-etched area only. Let dry. Use the Tourmaline outliner to outline each pink stripe up to the edge of the green circle. Let dry. On a separate plastic plate, mix three parts Peridot with one part Anthracite Black to create dark green. Using a fine paintbrush, paint a border on both the inside and outside edges of the green circle. Let dry. Turn the cake plate over to the serving side.

⋗ Designer's Tip ⋖

To create perfect painted stripes, I originally tried to use a masking technique by laying down strips of tape, painting between them, and then removing the tape. I found this terribly unsuccessful. When I removed the tape, the paint came with it in one big sheet. I thought perhaps I hadn't let it dry enough, so I tested it again. This time the paint along the edges cracked a bit with the tape removal, thus creating jagged edges. I recommend that hand painting, using a straightedge as a guide, will definitely yield the best results.

4. Using the Tourmaline outliner, draw two concentric circles on the top of the plate, about ⅜" apart where the foot meets the plate. Use the Marseilles Yellow outliner to create a wavy line within the circles. Next use the Tourmaline outliner to create dots over the pink stripes and use the Marseilles Yellow outliner to create dots over the green circle. Let dry. To write "Let them eat cake" on the checkerboard border, first practice on a piece of paper, using the Tourmaline outliner. Write the phrase five times around the edge of the plate, leaving about ½" between each phrase. When dry, use the Marseilles Yellow outliner to create a dot in the center of each non-etched square around the checkerboard border. To paint the bottom of the foot, mix three parts Ivory paint and one part Topaz on a plastic plate to create light pink. Paint a ⅜"-wide pink stripe around the base of the foot

using the flat paintbrush. When dry, apply a row of dots along the top and bottom edges of the stripe using the Tourmaline outliner. Let all the paint dry for at least 48 hours.

⇒ Designer's Tip ⇐

If you make a mistake of any kind or completely change your mind about what you've just painted, a little rubbing alcohol on a paper towel can undo all the damage. The best way to clean up small mistakes is to twist a piece of paper towel on the end of some pointy tweezers, dip it in alcohol, and use the point for precise paint removal. As long as the paint has not been baked, any design can be corrected.

5. Carefully remove all the cutouts. Use tweezers to press down on the painted edges while lifting off cutouts to prevent the paint from coming off with the cutouts. Use alcohol and a cotton swab to carefully remove any spray adhesive left behind. Bake the cake plate following the paint maufacturer's instructions. Take the plate out and allow it to cool. The design is now permanent. Place the plate, foot side up, on your kraft-paper work surface.

6. Remove five more strawberry cutouts from the packages of Wallies. On a plastic plate, mix equal parts of pink acrylic paint and Mod Podge. Apply the mixture to the back of all five cutouts, using a sponge brush. Let dry and repeat. Using a clean sponge brush, apply *only* Mod Podge to the front of one cutout and place it in its original position on the underside of the plate, so the image is visible through the glass on the front side. Smooth out any wrinkles or bubbles, and look at the plate from the serving side to ensure that all areas have adhered. Turn the plate back over to the footed side and clean up any stray glue using a damp paper towel. Repeat for the remaining four strawberry cutouts.

INSTRUCTIONS (FOR DOME)

1. Use glass cleaner to remove all grease and fingerprints from the glass. Run one length of ½"-wide masking tape around the outside bottom edge of the dome. Overlap the tape where the ends meet. Run a second length of tape around the dome directly above the first. Following the directions as in step 1 for the cake plate on page 52, make enough ½" squares to create two rows of a checkerboard pattern directly above the last length of tape applied to the dome. Run a length of tape around the dome above the checkerboard pattern so that the bottom edge of the tape touches the top edges of the tape squares. Apply a second length of tape around the dome above that. Now, remove the lengths of tape directly above and below the checkerboard rows only. These open areas will be etched. To protect the rest of the dome, add two more lengths of tape around the dome above the top row of tape. Apply etching cream over the checkerboard pattern and rinse thoroughly, removing the tape and following the manufacturer's directions.

2. Mix three parts Ivory paint and one part Topaz on a plastic plate to create light pink. Paint a ⅜"-wide stripe around the outside bottom edge of the dome using the ⅜" flat paintbrush. Let dry. Using the Tourmaline outliner, apply a row of dots along the top edge of the pink stripe all the way around the dome. Also, use this outliner to add dots on all non-etched squares and the Marseille Yellow outliner to create dots on all etched ones. Let dry at least 48 hours. Bake the dome following the paint manufacturer's instructions. Take the dome out and allow to cool. The design is now permanent.

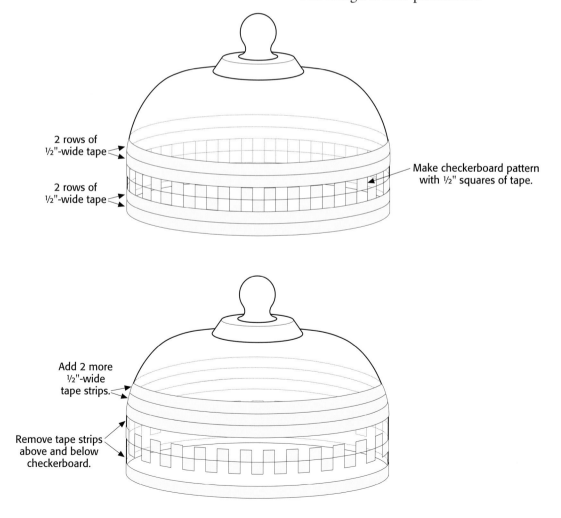

2 rows of ½"-wide tape

2 rows of ½"-wide tape

Make checkerboard pattern with ½" squares of tape.

Add 2 more ½"-wide tape strips.

Remove tape strips above and below checkerboard.

FLORAL PAPER LAMPSHADE

By Genevieve A. Sterbenz

Layers of pretty decorative papers and trim edging turn a plain lampshade into a beautiful accent for any room. This project features an allover patterned floral paper with hand-written rows of French text. The designer chose to write two French phrases: "J'aime beaucoup le printemps. Toutes les fleurs sont très jolies," which mean, "I really love the springtime. All the flowers are very pretty."

For best results, start with a shade that is very cylindrical rather than conical. The text is written on the decorative paper before the paper is applied to the shade, and it is much easier to write text in straight or nearly straight lines than to try to write rows of text that curve.

Trims were added to the exterior top and bottom of the shade, as well as to the interior to cover the raw edges of the paper. The center decorative accents maintain the color palette and floral theme created by the background paper and bring a central focus to the lampshade.

MATERIALS

- Cylindrical lampshade, 7" x 8" x 9"
- 12" x 28" sheet of floral decorative paper
- 12" x 28" piece of lightweight fusible interfacing
- Iridescent green gel pen (Gelly Roll)
- 1⅓ yards of soft green rose-and-pearl trim
- 1½ yards of pink-and-white polka dot grosgrain ribbon
- ¼ yard of pink satin ribbon (optional for back seam)
- 1 sheet of texturized iridescent pink paper
- Gold leaf sheets
- Magnolia image cut from wallpaper
- 3 pink flat-backed rhinestones, 4½ mm
- Brown or white packaging paper for pattern
- High-tack white glue
- Yes Stikflat Glue

TOOLS AND SUPPLIES

- Bristle brush
- Iron and ironing board
- Kraft paper
- Low-tack masking tape
- Newspaper
- Pencil
- Scissors
- Spray adhesive
- Straightedge
- Tape measure

Note: Because the floral paper used here was lightweight, it was laminated to lightweight fusible interfacing for added stability. If you are working with a heavy paper, you may choose to eliminate this step.

INSTRUCTIONS

1. Place the lampshade, seam side down, on kraft paper. Mark the paper at the upper and lower edges of the shade along the seam line. Roll the shade across the paper, tracing the upper and lower edges as you go, until the seam is reached again. Mark the paper at the seam as before. Remove the shade. Connect the upper and lower seam line marks at each end of the pattern. Add ½" to the upper and lower edges for a fold-over allowance and add 1" at the right end for overlap at the seam line. Cut out the pattern. Lay the decorative paper wrong side up on a work surface protected with kraft paper. Lay the pattern on the decorative paper and secure with tape. Trace around the pattern using a pencil. Remove the pattern and cut out the paper. Trace the pattern onto the fusible interfacing and cut out.

2. Lay the decorative paper, wrong side up, on an ironing board. Place the fusible interfacing, adhesive side down, on top of the paper. Following the manufacturer's directions, fuse the interfacing to the paper, adhering the two together. When cool, fold over the ½" hem on the top and bottom and the 1" hem on the right side. Turn back to the right side of the decorative paper and smooth flat.

3. Lay kraft paper on a protected work surface. Center the decorative paper on top and tape in place with the printed side up. Since the paper for the shade is slightly curved, use the following method to create a writing guide for straight lines. With your ruler along the right edge of the decorative paper, and starting at the top fold line, make a pencil mark on the edge of the decorative paper every ½". Repeat on the left edge. Then, lay the straightedge ruler vertically across the center of the decorative paper. Using an iridescent green pen, begin at the left edge of the paper, about ½" down from the fold line, and write: "J'aime beaucoup le printemps. Toutes les fleurs sont très jolies." Write toward the ruler, aiming for the mark ½" below the fold line. Move the ruler out of the way when you reach the center and continue writing and repeating the French phrase, aiming for the tick mark ½" below the fold line on the right side. Repeat this phrase as many times as necessary to reach the opposite side of the shade. Begin at the left edge again. Starting ½" below the first line of writing, reverse the order of the two parts of the phrase: "Toutes les fleurs sont très jolies. J'aime beaucoup le printemps." Continue writing the phrase in the same manner as the first line of text until you reach the opposite side of the shade. Continue writ-

ing in rows, spaced ½" apart, alternating the phrase order from row to row until the entire piece of decorative paper is completely covered with text.

⇛ DESIGNER'S TIP ⇚

If you are not comfortable handwriting text, consider writing only a few key words here and there, or purchase decorative papers that already have text on them to use as your background paper instead of the floral design. It is also possible to use photo transfer paper with text printed on it and iron it onto your background paper. It should be noted that the heat from the iron and the application of the transfer paper can alter the color of the background paper, so be sure to test a scrap piece before attempting this method on the shade itself.

4. Use the bristle brush to apply a thin, even coat of Yes Stikflat Glue to all outside surfaces of the lampshade, including the top and bottom edges and inside rims, following the manufacturer's directions. Lay the decorative paper on a protected work surface, wrong side up. Center one side of the lampshade on the paper. Lift the left side of the paper and press it to the lampshade, smoothing it flat with your hands. Repeat the process to adhere the right side of the paper to the lampshade. Lap the hem over the raw edge of the paper, using extra dabs of glue to adhere. Fold and finger-press the top and bottom edges to the inside rims of the shade. Set the shade aside.

5. Measure and cut two lengths of polka dot ribbon to fit around the inside rims of the lampshade at the top and bottom edges. (In the project shown, the pieces are 21" and 25" long.) Apply dabs of high-tack white glue along the raw edge of the paper where the decorative paper is wrapped to the inside of the shade at the top. Beginning at the top

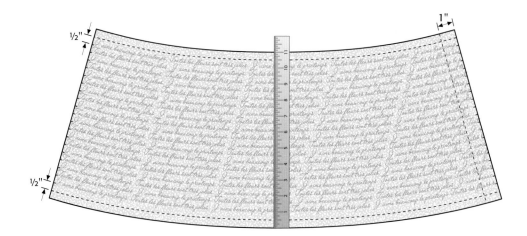

seam of the shade, position and press down one end of the shorter length of ribbon to adhere. Continue pressing ribbon around the inside edge of the shade until you reach the starting point. Trim the ribbon so the ends meet, as necessary. Repeat the process to glue the longer ribbon to the interior raw edge of the decorative paper at the bottom of the shade. If desired, measure and cut a 9" length of satin ribbon and glue it over the back outside seam line, trimming the ends flush with the top and bottom edges of the shade as necessary.

6. Measure and cut one length of rose-and-pearl trim for the top outer edge of the shade and two lengths of rose-and-pearl trim for the bottom outer edge of the shade. (The project shown uses one 22½" length and two 26½" lengths.) Apply dabs of white glue to the outside top edge of the shade. Beginning at the top of the shade's seam line, position and press down one end of the shorter length of trim. Wrap trim around the top edge of the shade until you reach the starting point, and cut the ends of the trim as necessary. Repeat the process on the bottom edge of the shade with the two longer lengths of trim. First apply trim to the bottom edge, and then apply the second length right above and touching the first.

7. On the pink iridescent paper, measure and mark a triangle with a base of 3" and a height of 6½". Carefully tear away the triangle, creating rough edges. It is not a problem if measurements change slightly. Lay the shade on your work surface, seam down. Center the triangle at an angle on the front of the shade and adhere with dabs of white glue. Do not adhere the edges of the triangle completely. Use a small loop of tape to temporarily center and position the magnolia cutout over the pink paper.

8. Add four arms of gold leaf to the collage, as if creating an X. To affix the gold leaf, begin at the upper left edge of the magnolia cutout and apply a thin, narrow triangle of white glue extending from the flower. Lift up that edge of the magnolia to apply glue so that the gold leaf appears to be coming from beneath the cutout. Lay gold leaf on the glued area and tamp down in place. Repeat to apply gold leaf to the remaining three "arms" of the X.

9. Remove the magnolia cutout and place face down on a protected work surface. Apply a light coat of spray adhesive to the cutout. Transfer the cutout to the shade, centering it over the existing pink paper and gold leaf collage. Use dabs of white glue to secure three flat-backed rhinestones to the magnolia cutout as shown in the project photo.

COLLAGE MAP TRAY

By Saralyn Ewald, Creative Coordinator, Archiver's: The Photo Memory Store

Decorate the interior of a ready-made tray with a collage of map papers and postcards, and then apply a few colorful stickers to create a stunning accent piece for your home. This tray features butterfly images, but you could also use floral cutouts or brightly colored postage stamps. To preserve the matte finish of the paper, it was left unsealed, but if you plan to use the tray as a serving piece, protect the paper images by placing a piece of cut-to-size glass over the inside of the tray and applying a couple of coats of clear sealer to the top edge to cover the map edging design.

MATERIALS

- Off-white serving tray, 10" x 16" interior dimensions
- Map-patterned paper (#0553 by Legacy Collage)
- 1 piece of ivory or off-white cardstock cut to fit inside tray (10" x 16" for the project shown)
- ScrappyChic Scrapbook Paper Collection (12" x 12"), Book 2, by Me and My Big Ideas
- 12" x 10" piece of tan antique map paper
- 4" x 10" piece of tan antique map paper
- 6¼" x 6¾" Alaska map (from the 12" x 12" ScrappyChic Scrapbook Paper Collection, Book 1, by Me and My Big Ideas)
- 8" x 8" Paris map (from the 8½" x 11" ScrappyChic Scrapbook Paper Collection, Book 1, by Me and My Big Ideas)
- 5¼" x 9⅛" piece of script paper (Isabella Script Printed Flat Paper by K and Company)
- 3 scraps, roughly 2" x 3", of bright white watercolor paper, cold press 140lb. (Arches)
- Gold Shadow Ink (Hero Arts)
- Studio Line Butterfly stickers (Mrs. Grossman's)
- Decorative Butterfly Stickers (Dover Publications)
- ScrappyChic Postmark Stickers by Me and My Big Ideas
- ScrappyChic Ephemera Assortments #2 and #8 by Me and My Big Ideas (includes post-cards, postage stamps, and foreign money)
- 4⅛" x 5⅜" piece of clear acetate
- Silver extra fine point metallic ink pen (Sakura)
- pH Neutral PVA Adhesive (Books By Hand)
- Super 77 Spray Adhesive (3M)

TOOLS AND SUPPLIES

- ◆ Cutter Bee Scissors (EK Success)
- ◆ Self-healing cutting mat
- ◆ X-Acto knife

INSTRUCTIONS

1. Coat one side of the piece of cardstock (cut to the interior tray dimensions) with spray adhesive, covering the paper without saturating it. Apply the two pieces of tan antique map paper to the cardstock, carefully covering the entire surface and positioning the paper flush with the edges of the cardstock.

2. Apply spray adhesive to the back of the Alaska map and adhere it flush with the top right corner of the map-covered cardstock.

3. Round off the edges of the script paper with scissors. Holding the gold ink pad open and upside down, lightly dab ink around the edges of the script paper to give it an antiqued appearance, applying more ink to the corners. Apply spray adhesive to the back of the inked paper and attach it flush with the bottom edge of the map-covered cardstock, positioning it about ½" from the left edge.

4. Apply spray adhesive to the back of a postcard (with red stamp). Position the postcard at a slight angle along the center of the bottom edge of the map-covered cardstock so that the bottom edge hangs off the cardstock.

5. At the top of the map-covered cardstock, use spray adhesive to attach foreign money. Position the bill about 1" from the left side of the cardstock with almost half of the money hanging off the cardstock.

6. Coat the back of the Paris map with spray adhesive and attach it at an angle toward the top left corner of the tray. Attach two brown-tone postage stamps to the upper right corner of the Paris map.

7. Apply the "Par Avion" sticker at the top of the map-covered cardstock, a scant ¼" to the right of the money.

8. Write a message in script using a silver marker on a sheet of clear acetate. Apply spray adhesive to the acetate, directly on the writing, and then turn the acetate over and adhere it to the map-covered cardstock, flush with the top edge and 4" from the right edge.

9. Coat the back of a postcard (with purple stamp) with spray adhesive. Attach the right edge of it flush with the right edge of the map-covered cardstock, approximately 1¼" from the top edge.

10. Spray the black-and-white decorative paper square with spray adhesive and position it approximately 2½" from the left edge and 2¼" from the bottom edge of the map-covered cardstock.

11. Flip the project over onto a self-healing cutting mat and trim off any overhanging elements with an X-Acto knife.

12. Apply three butterfly stickers to scraps of watercolor paper. Using fine-blade scissors, cut out the butterflies, leaving no watercolor border. Apply pH Neutral glue to the back of the largest butterfly. Adhere the butterfly at an angle, at the bottom left corner of the black-and-white decorative paper square. Position and adhere the second butterfly below the red stamp on the postcard, adhering it so more than half of the butterfly is to the right of the postcard. Adhere the third butterfly along the left edge of the postcard (with a purple stamp), about 1¾" from the top edge of the map-covered cardstock. Allow the glue to dry.

13. Apply spray adhesive to the back of the cardstock. Carefully secure the collage flush to the interior bottom of the tray.

14. Measure the width of the tray's edge. Using an X-Acto knife and self-healing cutting mat, cut six 12"-long strips of map-patterned paper to the determined width (5/16" in the project shown). Position two thin map strips along the top edge of one long side of the tray, butting the short ends of the strips together and keeping the long edges even with the edges of the tray. Allow the ends to hang off the sides. Trim off excess at the ends at 45° angles to create mitered corners. Glue in place with ph Neutral PVA Adhesive. Repeat on the opposite long edge of the tray. Glue the remaining strips of paper to the short edges of the tray, mitering the ends.

Collage Plan

DRAGONFLY GARDEN PAIL

By Christine Falk

Make a dragonfly garden pail for displaying large bouquets of flowers. This one is perfect for large or tall flowers like hydrangeas, snapdragons, delphiniums, and gladioli. Start with a plain galvanized bucket painted a glossy white. Add to the front a collage of items that carry out the dragonfly theme. The dragonfly and text were transferred to the bucket surface using Lazertran decal paper. The transfer paper designed for inkjet printers can be used with any printer that uses inks but not with toner-based printers.

MATERIALS

- Galvanized bucket with handles, approximate dimensions 7" x 12"
- White aerosol primer
- White aerosol glossy paint
- Clear aerosol acrylic sealer
- 3" x 3" piece of gray-tone patterned paper by Colorbök
- 3" x 3" piece of silver or gray vellum
- 8½" x 11" sheet of white cardstock
- Dragonfly image (from *Animals: 1,419 Copyright-Free Illustrations of Mammals, Birds, Fish, Insects, Etc. A Pictorial Archive from Nineteenth Century Sources*, by Jim Harter, Dover Publications)
- Gloss interior varnish (Delta Ceramcoat)
- Making Memories Charmed Photo Corners "twine" pattern
- Making Memories Charmed Plaque "dragonfly"
- Large dragonfly charm
- Beaded chain cut to 8" length
- 7-mm jump ring
- Liquid Leaf paint in Pewter
- Artsy Collage Decoupage and Collage Gel
- Craft glue dots
- Scotch Photo Laminating Sheet

TOOLS AND SUPPLIES

- Access to a color photocopier or access to a computer, inkjet printer, and scanner
- 8½" x 11" sheet of Lazertran waterslide decal paper for inkjet printers
- Drop cloth
- Fiskars Paper Edgers, deckle pattern
- Foam paintbrushes

- ◆ Pliers
- ◆ Sandpaper, 220-grit
- ◆ Scissors and/or paper cutter
- ◆ Small bowl
- ◆ Small paintbrush
- ◆ Tack cloth
- ◆ Wire cutters

⋝ DESIGNER'S TIPS ⋜

- Use several light coats of paint, rather than one heavy coat. This allows the paint to dry faster and prevents paint drips.

- If the paint does drip, wipe with a foam brush rather than a bristle brush to avoid leaving brush marks.

- Always follow the manufacturer's precautions when working with aerosols and spray the primer, paint, and acrylic sealer in a well-ventilated area.

INSTRUCTIONS

1. Cover your work surface with a drop cloth and place the galvanized bucket on the cloth. Lightly sand the outside and inside of the bucket and wipe away the sanding dust with a tack cloth.

2. Spray all surfaces with two light coats of primer. Let dry completely between coats.

3. Apply a light coat of white aerosol paint to the inside, outside, and bottom of the bucket. Apply two to three additional coats as necessary for complete coverage, allowing the paint to dry completely between each coat.

4. Apply clear aerosol acrylic sealer lightly over all painted surfaces of the bucket. Apply two to three more coats as necessary for even coverage, allowing the sealer to dry fully between each coat. Set the bucket aside.

5. Cover your work surface with a drop cloth and place the beaded chain and charm on the cloth. Apply Pewter paint to the charm and chain with a small paintbrush. Make sure the paint is applied evenly to achieve good coverage, especially when working with the chain.

6. If using a color photocopier, have the decorative text on page 69 copied onto the Lazertran inkjet paper at your local copy shop.

   If using a computer, either scan the text or use a word-processing program to type the words "La Libellule" (French for "dragonfly") and the poem "The dragonfly, so graceful and beautiful, visits my garden at the break of dawn." Use the English 111 Vivace BT font in 72-point size for "La Libellule" and change to 60-point size for the poem. Also type the dictionary definition of dragonfly found on page 69. For the definition, use the Arial font in 10-point size for all except the last word, for which use the Avant Garde font in 10-point size. Then print the text onto the Lazertran inkjet paper, following the manufacturer's directions. Allow to dry for one hour.

7. Trim closely around "La Libellule," around each word of the poem, and around the dictionary definition. Soak the text pieces in a bowl of hot water for about a minute until the words are released on decals. Immediately apply them to the bucket, referring to the project photo for placement. Allow to dry for 24 hours, and then apply gloss varnish to the decals with a foam brush.

8. Trim the edges of the two 3" x 3" pieces of paper (the patterned and the vellum) with the deckle paper edgers. Using a paintbrush or your fingertip, spread decoupage gel onto the back of the paper. Center the two squares on the front of the bucket as shown in the project photo, tilting the printed one slightly and overlapping it with the vellum one. Apply varnish over the two overlapped papers with a foam brush.

9. Photocopy or scan and print the dragonfly image onto cardstock. Cut the cardstock into a 3" x 3" square, keeping the dragonfly image in the center of the square. Allow the image to dry for one hour. Cut a 3" x 3" piece of photo laminating sheet and carefully place it on top of the dragonfly image, smoothing out bubbles. Once the laminating sheet is placed onto the cardstock, it cannot be removed. Apply decoupage gel to the back of the cardstock. Place on top of the overlapping squares already on the bucket, centering the image top to bottom and left to right.

10. Place one glue dot on the back of each pewter photo corner. Adhere the photo corners to the corners of the dragonfly image. Place four glue dots on the back of the pewter dragonfly plaque. Adhere the plaque to the front of the bucket at the lower right of the center dragonfly image.

11. To add the chain and charm, feed the jump ring through the loop at the top of the charm. Close the jump ring with pliers. Feed the chain through the jump ring. Hang the chain with the charm on the bucket handle.

La Libellule

The dragonfly, so graceful and beautiful, visits my garden at the break of dawn.

drag•on•fly \-,flī\ *n*: any of an order (Odonata) of large harmless insects that have four long wings and feed especially on flies, gnats, and mosquitoes — compare DAMSELFLY

STENCILED MIRROR FRAME

By Saralyn Ewald, Creative Coordinator, Archiver's: The Photo Memory Store

The soft palette used for this frame makes it a perfect accessory for a bedroom, bathroom, or anyplace needing a feminine touch. The collage incorporates scrapbooking papers, watercolor paper, dimensional design paste, ribbon, threads, and gold leaf. The focal point is a stenciled design created with dimensional design paste. The watercolor effect is achieved with the use of colored pencils that have been softened with water.

MATERIALS

- Mirror with wide, flat wooden frame, 10" x 10" outer dimensions
- Derwent Watercolor pencils in the following colors: Cedar Green 50, Pink Madder Lake 17, Golden Brown 59, Madder Carmine 19, Olive Green 51
- Tom Norton Designs Walnut Drawing Ink
- Liquitex Modeling Paste, Gel Medium
- American Traditional Stencils BL-697 Leaf Molding
- Bright white watercolor paper, cold press 140lb. (Arches)
- Scrap of cardstock or cardboard slightly larger than mirror
- Printed vellum with ivory and brown tones
- Striped scrapbooking paper (#4611 moss stripe paper from Sharon Soneff's Sonnets pattern by Creative Imaginations)
- Gold Pearl Ex Gilding Bitz
- 2-ply gold thread (New Metallics by On the Surface)
- ⅜ yard of gold satin ribbon, ¾" wide
- pH Neutral PVA Adhesive (Books By Hand)
- Scrappy Glue
- Super 77 Spray Adhesive (3M)
- Wonder Tape (Suze Weinberg)

TOOLS AND SUPPLIES

- Flat paintbrush
- Heavy books
- Masking tape
- Metal ruler
- Palette knife
- Pencil
- Self-healing cutting mat
- Small flat watercolor paintbrush
- Soft dry paintbrush
- Wax paper
- X-Acto knife

Instructions

1. Apply masking tape along the edges of the mirror where the mirror meets the wooden frame.

2. With a damp paintbrush, brush a 1½"-wide strip of pH Neutral PVA Adhesive evenly over the surface of the left side of the frame. Quickly position the moss stripe paper over the glue, making sure part of the pattern is within 1" of the outside edge of the frame. Smooth out any wrinkles or air bubbles. Once dry, turn the frame over and trim off the excess paper using an X-Acto knife.

3. Cut a piece of watercolor paper approximately 1" larger than the frame. In the project shown, the piece includes a natural edge of the paper for a softly frayed texture on the left edge. Using a palette knife, apply about a 5"-wide strip of modeling paste to the left side of the watercolor paper. Make sure you cover an area slightly larger than your leaf molding stencil. Smooth the layer of modeling paste with your palette knife, blending it into the paper at the right edge. Allow the paste to dry.

⇒ Designer's Tip ⇐

While your modeling paste is drying, clean off the stencil and palette knife. The modeling paste is more difficult to remove once it is dry.

4. Once dry, gently attach the leaf stencil over the pasted area, using masking tape to hold the stencil in place. Apply a liberal amount of modeling paste over the stencil, using the palette knife. Before the paste dries, carefully lift the stencil off the paper, revealing the raised design. Allow the paste to dry.

5. Once completely dry, color directly on the raised design using watercolor pencils. Use the pink tones for the bulk of the stencil, blending the two colors by using one over the other or

by graduating from one color to the next across the raised design. Use the green tones for the leaf shapes in the stencil, blending the two colors in the same manner. Add brown where desired to tone the colors down a bit. With a damp, but not wet, paintbrush, paint over your colored design with water to soften the colors and fill in the recessed areas.

6. Use the pink and brown watercolor pencils and a paintbrush to apply color to the rest of the paper in the same manner. Allow the colored wash to dry.

7. Once dry, use the small flat paintbrush to apply a wash of watered-down walnut ink over the painted paper, giving the colors a more antique feel.

⇒ Designer's Tip ⇐

You can blot the walnut wash with a paper towel as you apply it if the color is too strong in certain areas.

8. While the washed design is drying, cut a piece of cardstock or cardboard to the size of the mirror. Once the washed design is completely dry, position the cut cardstock square on top of the design, about where you would like the mirror to show through (leave about a 2" border on the left stenciled edge and a 3½" border on the remaining sides). Use a ruler to position the square accurately. Using a pencil, lightly trace the square on the design. Cut out the traced square using an X-Acto knife and a metal ruler.

9. With a slightly damp brush, apply pH Neutral PVA Adhesive evenly over the back of the stenciled piece. Position the piece on the mirror frame, aligning the opening with the mirror and pushing firmly on each edge to help the piece adhere to the wood. Place the project between two pieces of wax paper under a stack of heavy books, leaving in place for approximately 30 minutes to help it dry flat.

10. When dry, use an X-Acto knife and self-healing cutting mat to trim away the excess paper around the edges of the frame.

11. Apply a small amount of Scrappy Glue to some of the edges of the raised stencil design. Lay gold gilding flakes on top of the glue. Allow the glue to dry, then brush off the excess gilding flakes with a soft, dry paintbrush.

12. Apply strips of Wonder Tape to the edges of the wooden frame. Cover the tape with gilding flakes, gently brushing off the excess with a soft, dry brush. Repeat the taping and gilding process along the inside edge of the frame.

13. Cut a 1½" x 3½" rectangle of patterned vellum paper. Tear off a ¾" strip from one short end and discard. Using spray adhesive, attach the remaining piece to the right side of the mirror frame, about 1⅛" from the right edge, with the torn edge at the top and the bottom edge aligned with the bottom edge of the frame.

14. Wrap the gold satin ribbon around the right side of the frame, about ¼" to the right of the mirror, wrapping the ends around to the back of the frame. Secure with pH Neutral PVA Adhesive. Wrap two pieces of gold thread over the left half of the ribbon, spacing the fibers about ⅛" apart, and secure the ends in place on the back of the frame with masking tape.

Collage Plan

SEASHELL CANDLES

By Genevieve A. Sterbenz

Perfect for anyone who has a beach house or simply a love of the ocean, ordinary pillar candles can be transformed into beautiful accent pieces with decorative papers and a heat gun.

First a background paper is wrapped tightly around the candle. As heat is applied, the wax starts to melt and is absorbed into the paper, melding the surfaces together. The shell images are then added over the background papers and three-dimensional shells, feathers, beads, and sea glass add finishing touches.

As a general cautionary note, don't use trims around the top of a candle where they have a much greater chance of catching on fire. Never apply paper or embellishments to taper candles for the same reason. Also, never leave a burning candle unattended or place it on an uneven surface.

MATERIALS

- 2 white round pillar candles, 3" diameter x 3½" tall
- 1 white round pillar candle, 3" diameter x 5" tall
- White pillar candle, for melting wax
- Royal Coat Decoupage Paper Packs in the Anna Griffin Shells and Cockles design (Plaid item #2070)
- Artsy Collage Artsy Additions 3-D Collections in Tan (#HOTP 4305) and Blue (#HOTP 4303)
- High-tack white glue

TOOLS AND SUPPLIES

- Decoupage scissors
- Heat gun
- Panty hose
- Pencil
- Potholders
- Self-healing cutting mat
- Straight pins
- Straightedge
- Tweezers
- X-Acto knife

- Don't hold the heat gun on one area of the candle too long after the wax has started to melt. It could create a flat or dented area on the candle.

- Position the embellishments first using small bits of Fun-Tac adhesive to see if you like the arrangement before securing them in place permanently.

INSTRUCTIONS

1. On a self-healing mat, measure, mark, and cut one 3" x 8½" rectangle and one ½" x 3" rectangle from both the blue floral and script text papers. Also measure, mark, and cut one 5" x 8½" rectangle and one ½" x 5" rectangle from the blue striped paper.

2. Wrap blue floral paper around one 3½"-tall candle. The paper should be flush against the wax, with the long edges even with the top and bottom of the candle. The edges of the paper will not meet at the back of the candle. Secure the tops and bottoms of both ends with pins pushed gently into the wax. Place the smaller strip of blue floral paper on the back of the candle to cover the gap, and secure with pins. Repeat these steps to apply the script text paper to the second 3½" candle and the blue striped paper to the 5" candle.

3. Place a potholder on one hand and one candle on the potholder. Carefully wave the heat gun over the paper until the wax melts. The wax will saturate the paper and the paper will adhere to the candle. Continue to rotate the candle until all areas of the paper are adhered to the candle. Remove the pins. Repeat these steps on the remaining two candles.

4. Referring to the project photo, cut out shell images from the paper sheet using decoupage scissors. Place the candle for melting on a potholder placed on a flat surface. Place one shell image on the candle and hold in place with the tweezers. With the other hand, wave the heat gun over the shell until saturated with wax. Use the tweezers to peel the image off the candle and set aside. Repeat with the remaining shell images. Apply a thin even layer of white glue to the backs of the shell images and position and press them onto the candles, referring to the project photo for placement. When the glue is dry, smooth away drips and bring the covered candle surface to a high sheen by rubbing the candle with panty hose.

5. Use white glue and tweezers to apply sea glass, seashells, beads, and feathers to the candles as shown in the project photo, or as desired.

TRAVEL DESK BOX

By Genevieve A. Sterbenz

Create this handsome desk storage box to keep stationery and desk supplies neatly in order and concealed from view. Cover the wooden box with background papers and foreign travel images selected from three different books of collage papers.

The only added embellishment is a mock-closure created by gluing two foreign coins together. You could easily substitute a latch or lock-and-key hardware if you prefer.

MATERIALS

- Large cornice box, 12" wide x 9" deep x 3½" tall (Walnut Hollow #3213)
- Artsy Collage Travel Collage Kit (#HOTP 4202)
- Artsy Collage Travel Paper Art Images (#HOTP 4309)
- Artsy Collage Textured Papers Background Sheets (#HOTP 4310)
- White primer
- Grayish-blue acrylic paint
- 2 foreign coins of different sizes and colors
- High-tack white glue
- Matte finish decoupage glue
- 10" x 13" piece of felt

TOOLS AND SUPPLIES

- Decoupage scissors
- Kraft paper
- Paintbrush
- Paper towels
- Pencil
- Scissors
- Self-healing cutting mat
- Sponge brush
- Ruler
- Tweezers
- X-Acto knife

INSTRUCTIONS

1. Cover a clean, flat work surface with kraft paper. Apply one to two coats of primer to the inside and outside of the box, and let dry. Apply two coats of grayish-blue paint to the inside and outside of the box, allowing it to dry between coats. Choose four coordinating blue background papers and tear them out of the book. Position them on top of the box so that each paper covers one quarter of the top surface. Allow the excess paper to hang over the outside edges of the box. Apply a light coat of decoupage glue to the back of one paper using a sponge brush. Put the paper back in its original position and smooth flat with your hands. Repeat for the remaining three papers. When dry, run an X-Acto knife along the edge of the box to trim away the excess paper.

2. Search through the Artsy Collage travel books for desired images, using the collage plan on page 80 and the project photo as a guide. Cut out the images using decoupage scissors. Arrange the images on top of the box. Once the desired arrangement is achieved, apply glue to the back of one image and replace it in its original position, using tweezers to aid you. Continue gluing the images to the surface until completely covered. Once dry, use an X-Acto knife to remove any excess paper hanging over the outside edges of the box.

3. Choose coordinating papers for the side edges of the lid and the base of the box and tear them out of the book. You need one style for the lid and three styles for the base. Place the chosen paper for the lid edges, horizontally, on a self-healing cutting mat. Measure, mark, and cut five strips of paper, each 1" wide, using the full length of the paper. Stand the box up so the front side is facing up. Begin at the front center point of the lid. Position one strip of paper to the right of the center point and one to the left. Do not overlap the papers. Simply butt the ends up against each other, leaving no space in between. Be sure the top edges are flush with the top edge of the box. Apply light coats of decoupage glue to the backs of the strips and glue in place. If there is a slight overhang, be sure it is on the bottom edge. When dry, trim away the excess using an X-Acto knife. Continue rotating the box and adding the remaining strips of paper to the sides of the lid, and then let dry. Rotate the box so the back is facing up. Position two strips of matching paper on the back lid of the box. Once the paper is in place, push one strip of paper up against the hinge until a dented outline is created. Use an X-Acto knife to trim away the excess paper along the created line. Apply glue to the back of the paper and put it back in place. The hinge should be showing. Repeat for the opposite side and hinge. Place the papers for the base of the box on a self-healing cutting mat and cut six strips (two strips in each style) of paper 2¼" wide, using the full length of the paper. Stand the box up so the front side is facing up. Begin at the center point and apply two matching strips of paper on the front of the box. Trim away the excess while the glue is still wet, using decoupage scissors after the corner is covered, and then let dry. Apply two matching papers on the short ends of the box in the same manner. Rotate the box so that the back is facing up. Position two strips of matching paper on the back of the box. Mark and trim away the excess at the hinges as for the lid. Glue the papers in place.

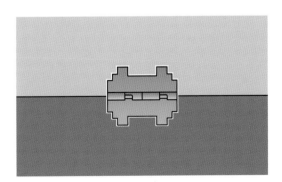

4. Choose papers to line the inside bottom of the box and trim to size. Apply glue to the backs of the papers and position in place. Let the glue dry.

5. Using a sponge brush, apply a light coat of decoupage glue to the outside and inside of the box, and let dry.

6. Use white glue to adhere the smaller coin in the center of the larger one, and then let dry. Place the box on your work surface with the front side facing up. Let the lid fall open slightly and use a heavy book to hold the box in position. Center the coins on the front edge of the box lid with three-quarters of the layered coins on the lid and one-quarter overhanging the lid. Glue the coins in place, using white glue. Let dry.

7. Place the felt on the work surface, and place the box on the felt. Trace around the box using a pencil and cut out with scissors. Apply a light coat of white glue to the bottom of the box. Position the felt on the bottom of the box with the edges even. Smooth flat with your hands.

Collage Plan

LOVE LETTER PILLOW

By Genevieve A. Sterbenz

All the elements of a love letter—elegant text, an envelope, and a pretty rose postage stamp complete with a postmark—come together in this collage. The center, is created by layering a variety of papers, and then the design is photo-transferred onto fabric. Finally the panel is accented with charms, rhinestones, beads, and a mini fabric envelope.

The "love" lettering and mottled rose border on the collage are most easily created by using a computer and graphics program. However, if you don't have access to a computer, you could add the lettering with rubber alphabet stamps and create a similar mottled rose border using a marker.

MATERIALS

- ½ yard of pale pink silk shantung
- ⅓ yard of cream polished cotton
- 14" square pillow form
- 2 yards of aqua blue pom-pom fringe
- Matching thread
- 8½" x 11" sheet of parchment paper
- 8½" x 11" sheet of paper with French text (European Country Collage Papers by DMD Industries)
- 2 sheets of 8½" x 11" white cardstock
- 8½" x 11" sheet of aqua blue cardstock
- 8½" x 11" sheet of rose cardstock
- Charms: large cherub, small cherub, ¼" heart, and ½" heart

- Scrap of aqua blue ribbon, about ⅛" wide
- 5-mm pale lavender bead
- 1 clear, size 11 seed bead
- 8-mm rose bead
- 5-mm flat-backed crystal rhinestone
- 1-cm flat-backed sapphire blue rhinestone
- Pink and aqua metal paints
- Coin, about 1" in diameter
- Glue stick
- Permanent beading glue
- Rose-colored marker

TOOLS AND SUPPLIES

◆ Access to a color photocopy machine or access to a computer, color printer, scanner, and graphics software package

◆ Beading needle

◆ Clear grid ruler

◆ Decoupage scissors

◆ Hand-sewing needle

◆ Iron and ironing board

◆ Pencil

◆ Rotary cutter

◆ Scissors

◆ Self-healing cutting mat

◆ Sewing machine

◆ Small paintbrush

◆ Straight pins

◆ X-Acto knife

◆ Zipper foot attachment for sewing machine

INSTRUCTIONS

1. On a clean, flat work surface, measure, mark, and cut two 15" squares from silk shantung. Set aside. Measure, mark, and cut one 8½" x 9¼" rectangle and one 3" x 8" rectangle from cotton. Press the four cut pieces of fabric with a hot iron and set aside.

2. If using a computer and scanner, follow steps 2–4. (If you don't have access to a computer, see the Designer's Tip on page 84.) Scan the parchment paper. The parchment paper image will be used as both a border around the love letter and as a pocket envelope. Using the parchment image, create one document to be used for the pocket envelope. For the border around the love letter, tear the original sheet of parchment paper to measure 4¾" x 5". Create a wavy rose border by coloring the torn edges of the paper with the rose marker. Using a self-healing mat, a ruler, and an X-Acto knife, measure, mark, and cut a 3¼" x 4½"

vertical rectangle from text paper, a 3⅜" x 4⅝" rectangle from aqua cardstock, and a 3½" x 4¾" rectangle from rose cardstock. With the glue stick, apply glue to the back of the text paper. Center and adhere it to the aqua rectangle. Apply glue to the back of the aqua paper, and center and adhere it to the rose rectangle. Apply glue to the back of the rose paper, and center and adhere it to the parchment paper, smoothing flat with your hands. Apply glue to the back of the parchment paper and adhere it to the plain white paper, leaving at least a 1" border on the right, top, and bottom edges. Set the layered papers aside.

3. Photocopy or scan and print out onto white cardstock the rose postage stamp on page 85. Use decoupage scissors to cut around the stamp just outside the marked line, simulating a perforated edge. Place the layered papers on your work surface in a vertical position. Apply glue with glue stick to the wrong side of the postage stamp and adhere it ¼" from the upper left corner of the parchment, letting ½" extend past the left edge of the parchment paper and onto the plain white paper. To make the postage mark, position the coin with its right edge over the left edge of the postage stamp. Using a pencil, trace around the coin. Lift the coin off the paper. Referring to the guide on page 85 for the postmark, use the pencil to write the date, time, and place within the circle. Draw six wavy lines extending from the right edge of the circle over the postage stamp, ending on the text paper.

4. Scan the image into a computer. Use a graphics program to add "LOVE" in rose and aqua blue colors, diagonally across the scanned papers, using the Parchment font in 108-point size. Using a graphics program, blend the wavy rose border into the outer edge of the parchment border, if desired, using a smudge tool. Create a mirror image and follow the manufacturer's directions to print the image onto photo transfer paper. Trim away the

excess paper on all sides and set aside. For the envelope, print out the original scanned image of the parchment paper on a second piece of transfer paper. Place it on a self-healing mat. Measure, mark, and cut a 2½" x 7½" rectangle from the transfer paper and set aside.

⇒ Designer's Tip ⇐

If you don't have access to a computer, scanner, and printer, you can achieve similar results with a copy machine. First, follow the manufacturer's directions to photocopy the parchment paper onto photo transfer paper, trim a 2½" x 7½" rectangle from the photo transfer paper, and set aside to use later for the envelope pocket. Then create the layered paper collage as in steps 2 and 3 on page 83 and photocopy the design onto photo transfer paper, following the manufacturer's instructions. With this method you will need to add the "LOVE" lettering later. Continue as in step 5. Then to add the "LOVE" letters, use rubber alphabet stamps about 1" to 1¼" tall to spell out the word "LOVE," using aqua or rose-colored ink. Finish the pillow following steps 6–9.

5. Press under ¼" hems on the outer edges of the larger rectangle of cotton fabric. Turn the fabric to the right side and center the photo transfer with the layered paper design, wrong side up, on the center of the cream cotton. Following the manufacturer's directions, press with a dry iron set on cotton or the highest setting. Run the iron over the entire surface area, paying close attention to all edges. Carefully lift off the paper backing. Transfer papers vary in terms of when to remove the backing paper (that is, when the image is still hot, or after it has cooled), so read the directions carefully. Set aside.

6. Transfer the remaining parchment image for the envelope onto the 3" x 8" piece of cotton in the same manner. Trim the cotton to 2½" x 7½", even with the edges of the transferred image. Place the 2½" x 7½" cotton rectangle, wrong side up, in a vertical position on your

work surface. Measure and mark the rectangle into three equal squares, making tick marks every 2½" along both long sides, and then draw two horizontal lines across the rectangle, connecting the tick marks. Fold the bottom square up and the top square down. Unfold. On the top square only, measure and mark midpoints on the top and sides, using a pencil. Then draw lines from the side midpoints to the top midpoint. Trim away the corners of the original square by cutting along the lines.

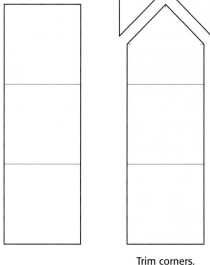

Trim corners.

Turn the unfolded envelope to the right side. Stitch ⅛" from all edges, using a sewing machine. Set aside.

7. Place one square of silk shantung right side up on your work surface. Position the cream cotton with the photo transfer in the center of the shantung square, using straight pins to secure. Stitch ⅛" from the folded edges of the cotton rectangle. Refold the envelope with the pointed flap on top. Position the envelope in the lower right corner of the center design and pin in place. Lift up the pointed flap and stitch around the sides and bottom over the previous stitching. Bring the flap down.

8. Lay the pillow cover front, right side up, on your work surface. Position and pin the fringe heading (the flat woven band) of the pom-pom

fringe along all four outside edges of the shantung square, clipping into the fringe heading at the corners as necessary for it to lie flat. The pom-poms should face into the center of the pillow front. Overlap the fringe where the ends meet. Secure pom-poms in place with straight pins to avoid catching them in your sewing needle. Machine stitch along the inner edge of the fringe heading, approximately ½" in from the edge with the zipper foot.

Stitch fringe heading to pillow front along inner edge of fringe heading. Clip fringe heading at corners.

Position the pillow front and back with right sides together and raw edges even; pin. Machine stitch around all sides just over the previous stitching, leaving an opening for turning and being careful not to sew over the pom-poms. Clip the corners and turn to the right side. Insert the pillow form and slip-stitch the opening closed.

9. Using the small paintbrush, apply a small amount of pink and aqua paint around the outer edge of the large cherub charm and allow to dry. Attach two small heart charms to a jump ring and attach to the loop of the large cherub charm. Tie the aqua blue ribbon in a bow around the loop of the large cherub charm. Hand stitch the ribbon bow to the top edge of the envelope at the center, using a threaded needle. Using a beading needle, take a stitch through the point of the envelope flap from back to front. Thread the needle through the lavender bead, then through the clear seed bead, and back through the lavender bead to the back of the flap, and knot to secure. Trim the thread. Hand stitch the small cherub charm and the pink bead near the postage stamp and post mark, as shown. Use beading glue to adhere the flat-backed rhinestones in place.

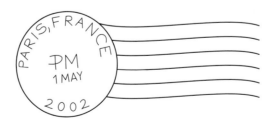

TRAVEL COASTERS

By Debba Haupert, BoBella Marketing & Design

Next time you entertain, enjoy using these travel coasters with their sepia-tone photos and vintage charm. Create these interesting coasters by transferring photo images onto marble tiles. You can use your own travel photos to personalize your coasters or photocopy images like the ones shown here from a copyright-free publication.

MATERIALS

- 4 tumbled marble tiles, 4" x 4"
- 4 photo images (from *Photo Archive of Famous Places of the World* by Donald M. Witte, Dover Publications)
- 8" x 8" sheet of cork (about ¹⁄₁₆" to ⅛" thick)
- Envirotex Lite gloss finish
- Glass, Metal and More permanent premium glue (Beacon)
- White glue

TOOLS AND SUPPLIES

- Access to a color photocopy machine
- Access to a computer, color printer, scanner, and graphics software package (optional)
- 2 sheets of 8½" x 11" Lazertran waterslide decal paper (regular)
- Box for covering coasters while drying (optional)
- Clear tape
- Sandpaper, coarse grit (optional)
- Craft knife
- Foam brush
- Heat gun (or oven)
- Plastic cups
- Scissors
- Shallow box or plastic for work surface
- Wooden craft stick

INSTRUCTIONS

1. If using a photocopy machine, trim your images to squares and resize them as necessary to measure ¼" larger than the tiles all around. Photocopy the images in color onto the Lazertran paper in reverse, two images per sheet, following the manufacturer's directions. (Even if the photo is in black and white, a color photocopy will give the image more depth than using a one-color or black copier.) To add text, see the tip on page 88.

   If using a computer, scan your photo images. Resize the images as necessary to measure ¼" larger than the tiles all around. To add text, use a graphics software package to add the name of the location in white to the front of each image, referring to the project photo for text placement. Print the images in reverse. Then photocopy the images in color onto the Lazertran paper, two images per sheet, following the manufacturer's directions. (Even if the photo is in black and white, a color photocopy will give the image more depth than using a one-color or black copier.) Some photocopiers produce shiny images on Lazertran, some do not. If your copied images are dull, the toners are probably not heat set. To do so, blow hot air on the paper with a heat gun. Hold over the image until the toners become shiny. Continue over the images until all areas covered with toner are heat set. If you don't have a heat gun, you can also set the toner in an oven following the directions on the Lazertran packaging.

⋛ DESIGNER'S TIP ⋹

If you don't have access to a computer, scanner, and printer, you can create coasters like these with just a photocopier. Simply photocopy your black-and-white or sepia-tone images in color onto the Lazertran paper following the manufacturer's instructions. Then to add text, write on top of the decal with permanent ink pens. Metallic or white markers create beautiful results.

2. Cut out the decals and soak in water. While soaking, apply a small amount of white glue to the surface of the tile and spread with a damp foam brush. Slide a decal off its backing sheet onto the glue surface. Put a small amount of glue on top of the decal and smooth out any air bubbles with the wet foam brush. Trim along the edges of the tile with a craft knife to give a slightly uneven appearance to the edges. Repeat for the remaining tiles, and allow to dry.

3. Paint another layer of glue over each decal image with the wet foam brush and allow to dry again. Note: The Envirotex Lite added in Step 5 may bead up on Lazertran if the additional layer of glue does not completely cover the surface. Make sure all areas of the tiles are covered, or apply an additional coat to assure complete coverage. Apply clear tape to the back of each tile along the sides.

4. Using a plastic cup and a wooden craft stick, mix the Envirotex Lite per the manufacturer's directions. Place the tiles (image side up) on inverted plastic cups in a protected area (inside a well-sealed box or over a covered area so that the drips do not adhere to anything that can't be discarded). Make sure the cups are on a flat surface.

5. Pour the Envirotex Lite mixture onto the tiles. Be sure to cover the tiles completely and allow excess to seep over and cover the edges of the tile. Use a craft stick to smooth the Envirotex Lite evenly over the side edges of the tiles. Allow to cure for 24 to 48 hours. (Time required depends on the temperature and humidity.) You may want to cover the project with a box to protect it from dust.

6. Once completely dry, remove the tape from the back of the tiles. Any drips that do not come off with the tape can be sanded off or carefully cut from the tiles with a craft knife.

7. Using scissors, cut the cork sheet to fit the bottom of a tile, and glue in place with Glass, Metal, and More permanent premium glue. Repeat for each tile. Allow to dry completely.

⋛ DESIGNER'S TIPS ⋹

• For a variation on the travel coasters shown here, try layering decal images over each other (note that white areas will be transparent).

• Make a set of tiles that create one large image when fit together, but that can still be used and enjoyed as separate coasters.

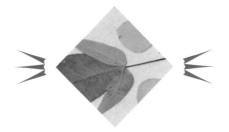

Leaf Collage Side Table

By Nancy Overton

Add interest to a plain wooden side table by creating a botanical collage design on the top. Collect an assortment of leaves, press them flat in a book until dried, and then glue them to a piece of rice paper mounted over a double paper mat that creates the borders around the design. To protect your collage, cover the surface of the table with a piece of glass cut to fit.

To press leaves for the project, collect and place them between the pages of a large book such as a thick phone directory. Weight the book with other large heavy books. Most of the leaves will be dry and ready to use in one to two weeks. If you are making a square table and want all four quadrants to be the same, be sure to collect your leaves in multiples of 4, such as 4, 8, 12, or 16 leaves of a particular species.

MATERIALS

- Wooden side table, 22¾" square
- 20" x 20" piece of tan art paper
- 19" x 19" piece of pale sage green art paper
- 16" x 16" piece of off-white watercolor paper
- 16" x 16" piece of off-white rice paper
- Assorted dried, pressed leaves
- 22¾" square piece of glass, ¼" deep with polished edges

TOOLS AND SUPPLIES

- Double-stick tape
- Elmer's Glue-All
- Mat knife
- Metal ruler
- Pencil
- Sponge brush

Instructions

1. Fold up 1⅛" on each side of the rice paper square. Hand-tear the rice paper along the fold lines to make a 13¾" x 13¾" square.

2. Dilute the white glue with water until it is the thickness of heavy cream. Using the sponge brush, apply the glue to the watercolor paper, keeping a 1⅛" border without glue around the edges. Place the rice paper in the center of the watercolor paper. Use the sponge brush or your fingers to lightly press away any air bubbles. Smooth the paper flat around the edges to secure. Let the paper dry completely. It may warp slightly, but will be pressed flat under the glass later.

3. Measure and mark the center of the rice paper lightly with a pencil. If desired, also lightly mark the centers of the side edges of your paper to use as a guide for keeping your arrangement symmetrical. Referring to the project photo for inspiration, arrange your design on the rice paper, using your pressed leaves. Use your pencil marks and the four corners of the paper as guides for placing the leaves evenly on all four sides. When satisfied with the arrangement, lift one leaf at a time, turn over, and apply full-strength (undiluted) glue with your finger or the sponge brush to the back. Return the leaf to its original position on the rice paper and press in place. Repeat with each leaf until all leaves are secured in place. Let dry thoroughly.

⋑ Designer's Tip ⋐

You can create heart shapes as shown below by simply overlapping two burgundy petal-shaped leaves to create the two sides of the heart.

4. Center the tan paper on the tabletop with about 1½" around all edges and secure in place with double-stick tape. Center the pale green paper over the tan paper, leaving a ½" border of tan on all sides. Secure in place with double-stick tape. Center the collage on the pale green paper, leaving a 1½" border of pale green on all sides. Secure in place at the midpoint of each side and at the corners with double-stick tape.

5. Position the glass top over the collage design.

FRAMED CHICKEN AND ROOSTER COLLAGES

By Saralyn Ewald, Creative Coordinator, Archiver's: The Photo Memory Store

These framed chicken and rooster designs with their retro charm are perfect to hang in a kitchen. A variety of torn papers are overlapped to create the backgrounds for the designs. Then, tags stained with walnut ink are used as surfaces for mounting the chicken and rooster images, which came from a decoupage paper collection. Ephemera labels, aged typewriter key stickers, and vintage buttons add the finishing touch.

To add even more dimension to the collage, use cardboard as a backing for the tags, labels, and chicken images. It helps each of the items stand out just a bit, adding more texture to the collages.

MATERIALS

- 5" x 7" whitewashed picture frame
- 7" x 7" white picture frame
- Roosters and Hens decoupage papers (Plaid)
- 7 Gypsies walnut-washed tags, 2⅜" x 4¾"
- ScrappyChic Ephemera Assortments 3 and 11 (Me and My Big Ideas)
- Small-scale black gingham paper (The Paper Patch)
- Legacy Collage shorthand paper #0549
- Scrap Ease large leaf: white pepper paper
- Anna Griffin paper AG050 (red flourish)
- Cardboard or heavy watercolor paper scraps
- 2 sheets of 8½" x 11" light-colored cardstock
- "Aged Typewriter" ABC stickers by Stickopotamus/Rebecca Sower Designs
- "Rule of Thumb" stickers by Stickopotamus/Rebecca Sower Designs
- 3 vintage plastic buttons:
    - ⅝" red button for chicken collage
    - ½" blue button for rooster collage
    - ¾" red button for rooster collage
- Scrap of light blue gingham fabric
- 6" length of ⅜"-wide red gingham ribbon (May Arts)
- Clipiola Italian paperclip
- Small gold safety pin, ¾" long
- White sewing thread
- pH Neutral PVA Adhesive (Books By Hand)
- Hermafix Transfer Adhesive
- Wonder Tape (Suze Weinberg)

TOOLS AND SUPPLIES

- ◆ Cutter Bee Scissors (EK Success)
- ◆ ¼" hole punch
- ◆ Scissors
- ◆ Self-healing cutting mat
- ◆ X-Acto knife

⇒ DESIGNER'S TIP ⇐

When adhering a large piece of paper, use a dry adhesive, such as Hermafix Transfer Adhesive, to prevent the paper from the rippling and curling that can result from using liquid glue.

INSTRUCTIONS
(FOR 5" X 7" CHICKEN COLLAGE)

1. Cut light-colored cardstock to fit inside the 5" x 7" frame. This will serve as the background for creating the collage. Cover the cardstock with shorthand patterned paper, attaching it to the cardstock with Hermafix Transfer Adhesive.

2. Tear a triangle with 3" sides from the corner of the black gingham paper and adhere to the lower left corner of the design with Hermafix Transfer Adhesive.

3. Cut a 2⅜" x 3" piece of red flourish paper and adhere to one of the walnut-washed tags about 1" down from the upper edge, using Hermafix Transfer Adhesive. Trim the tag ⅛" below the lower edge of the red flourish paper.

4. Cut a 1" square of blue gingham fabric and pull out a couple of threads along one side. Adhere the fabric square to the upper right corner of the tag, using Wonder Tape. Wrap white thread several times through the holes of the red button and tie the ends in a knot on the top. Trim the thread tails to about ⅜" long. Secure the button to the gingham fabric square with Wonder Tape. Attach the small safety pin through the hole of the tag.

5. Using scissors or an X-Acto knife, carefully cut a chicken image from a decoupage sheet. Cut cardboard scraps to fit behind the chicken and glue in place with pH Neutral PVA Adhesive. Glue the chicken to the tag so that the head extends slightly off the top of the tag at the upper left corner.

6. Punch a hole at the top of the round Orangeade ephemera label. Fold the piece of red gingham ribbon in half and insert the ends through the hole in the label from the back. Then push the ends through the loop at the folded end of the ribbon and pull snug. Trim the thread tails at an angle, cutting one end of the ribbon slightly longer than the other. Cut a scrap of cardboard to fit behind the round Orangeade ephemera label and adhere in place on the back of the label with pH Neutral PVA Adhesive.

7. Using Wonder Tape, adhere the Orangeade label to the lower left corner of the background paper, with almost half of the label overlapping the black gingham paper. Using

Wonder Tape, adhere the chicken tag to the background paper about 1⅝" from the left edge of the background and 1⅜" below the top edge of the background.

8. Using the typewriter key stickers, spell out the word "EGGS" in the lower left corner of the collage. Insert the collage into the frame.

INSTRUCTIONS
(FOR 7" X 7" ROOSTER COLLAGE)

⋟ DESIGNER'S TIP ⋞

To give a weathered look to a glossy painted frame, sand the details and edges of the frame with medium-grit sandpaper.

1. Cut light-colored cardstock to fit inside the 7" x 7" frame. This will serve as the background for creating the collage. Cover the cardstock with white leaf-patterned paper, attaching it to the cardstock with Hermafix Transfer Adhesive.

2. Tear off a corner of the red flourish paper with the left edge of the triangle measuring about 5" long and the bottom edge measuring about 2" long. Tear off a 7½"-long strip from the shorthand patterned paper with the strip measuring about 1¼" wide at the top and 2¼" wide at the bottom. Adhere the torn papers to the white leaf-patterned paper, using Hermafix Transfer Adhesive. Position the red flourish triangle in the lower left corner and the shorthand patterned paper along the right edge.

3. Cover the bottom third of a walnut-washed tag with black gingham paper, using Hermafix Transfer Adhesive. Run a segment of a ruler sticker across the top edge of the gingham paper.

4. Using the circle paper clip, clip a circular green ephemera label to the upper right corner of the tag.

5. To add dimension, cut strips of cardboard scraps and adhere them to the back of the decorated tag, as well as to the back of a second walnut-washed tag, using pH Neutral PVA Adhesive.

6. Carefully cut a rooster image from the decoupage paper and adhere cardboard scraps to the back of the image.

7. Position the blank tag on the background surface about ¾" from the left edge and 1" from the top edge. Position the decorated tag about ¼" to the right, aligning the edges. Secure the tags in place with Wonder Tape. Secure the rooster over the blank tag so that it overlaps the decorated tag. Trim the tail feathers as necessary so they will be even with the edge of the assembled frame.

8. Wrap white thread several times through the holes of the red and blue buttons and knot the ends on top. Trim the thread tails to about ⅜" long. Secure the buttons, using Wonder Tape, to the lower left corner of the left tag, below the rooster as shown in the project photo.

9. Add an aged typewriter key sticker to the bottom left corner of the right tag. Insert the collage into the frame.

Sources

Beacon Adhesives Company
914-699-3400, fax: 914-699-2783
www.beaconadhesives.com
Fabri-Tac Permanent Adhesive; Glass, Metal, and More permanent premium glue
("La Vie En Rose" Pillow, page 27; La Cucina Clock, page 47; Travel Coasters, page 87)

Dover Publications, Inc.
800-223-3130
Books with copyright-free photos and designs for artists, sticker books
(Butterfly Bath Chest, page 19; Rose Engravings Table Runner, page 23; Collage Map Tray, page 63; Dragonfly Garden Pail, page 67; Travel Coasters, page 87)

Environmental Technology, Inc.
707-443-9323, fax: 707-443-7962
www.eti-usa.com
Envirotex Lite
(Travel Coasters, page 87)

Hot Off The Press
800-227-9595
email: info@hotp.com
www.craftpizazz.com
Collage paper books, 3-D collections embellishments (Note: Artsy Collage from Hot Off The Press is available through the Paper Wishes direct-to-consumer catalog.)
(Seashell Candles, page 75; Travel Desk Box, page 77)

Lazertran Waterslide Decal Papers
800-245-7547, fax: 516-488-7898
email: lazertran@msn.com
www.lazertran.com
Lazertran photo transfer papers
(Mosaic Candle Luminary, page 41; Dragonfly Garden Pail, page 67; Travel Coasters, page 87)

Plaid Enterprises, Inc.
800-842-4197
www.plaidonline.com
Collage papers, acrylic paint, mosaic supplies and tools
(Mosaic Mirror with Shelf, page 13; Mosaic Candle Luminary, page 41; Cabbage Rose Charger Plate and Napkin Ring, page 33; Seashell Candles, page 75; Framed Chicken and Rooster Collages, page 93; La Cucina Clock, page 47)

Wallies Wallpaper Cutouts
800-255-2762, ext. 373
www.wallies.com
Wallpaper cutouts
(La Cucina Clock, page 47; "Let Them Eat Cake" Cake Plate and Dome, page 51)

Walnut Hollow
800-950-5101
www.walnuthollow.com
Clock-making parts
(La Cucina Clock, page 47; Travel Desk Box, page 77)

Wits End Mosaic
480-456-0364, fax: 480-456-0365
www.mosaic-witsend.com
Ceramic leaves, glass gems, mosaic supplies
(Mosaic Mirror with Shelf, page 13)